Road Cash

How to earn money on the road

by

William Myers

www.bmyers.com

Disclaimer

The information in this book is based on the author's knowledge, experience, and opinions. The methods described in this book are not intended to be a definitive set of instructions. You may discover other methods and materials to accomplish the same result. Your results may differ.

There are no representations or warranties, express or implied, about the completeness, accuracy, or reliability of the information, products, services, or related materials contained in this book. The information is provided "as is," to be used at your own risk.

This book is not intended to give legal or financial advice and is sold with the understanding that the author is not engaged in rendering legal, accounting or other professional services or advice. If legal or financial advice or other expert assistance is required, the services of a competent professional should be sought to ensure you fully understand your obligations and risks.

This book includes information regarding the products and services of third parties. We do not assume responsibility for any third-party materials or opinions. Use of mentioned third party materials does not guarantee your results will mirror those mentioned in the book.

All trademarks appearing in this book are the property of their respective owners.

This book may not be re-sold or given away to other people. If you would like to share this book with another person, please purchase an additional copy for each person you share it with.

Version 2017.06.08

Table of Contents

Introduction

It's a dream shared by many. Traveling the country in a recreational vehicle or camper, chasing good weather and visiting all the places on your bucket list. Leaving the nine to five world behind, saying 'goodbye' to the boss and living full time on the road.

The problem – for most of us anyway – is being able to afford it. It costs money to live on the road.

While it is true you can significantly reduce your overhead by selling off everything and moving into an RV, you'll still have expenses to cover. Paying for food, fuel, campground fees, insurance, and vehicle maintenance can add up.

At a minimum, it'll cost most people several hundred dollars a month or more to live out of a camper or RV. This assumes very little travel (and fuel expenses), sticking with low-cost or free campsites, preparing your own meals and complying with state licenses and insurance regulations.

If you like to travel a lot and spend time (and money) at various attractions, your monthly costs will climb significantly.

But, as proven by the hundreds of thousands of people who are living on the road these days, it can be done – even on a tight budget. Especially if you know how to earn money while on the road.

That's what this book is all about – showing you different ways to make money while traveling in your RV or camper.

Some of the methods require a computer and internet connection. Others require nothing more than a willingness to stay in one place for a few months. Some involve manual labor or crafting skills, while others only that you have a bit of luck.

As you'll discover within the pages of this book, there are many ways to legally earn money while living on the road. And while not every method will appeal to you, chances are you'll find several that will.

Having more than one way to make money while on the road is important, because you never know when income from one source might dry up. When that happens (and it will), you'll want to be able to fall back on other ways to generate cash.

That's why I recommend you pursue a flexible, multi-tiered approach to generating income. That way, if the cash flow from one of your efforts drops off, you'll have others to fall back on.

I suggest that as you read this book, you make a list of the income generating options that you and your traveling companions find interesting or fun.

Start with the ones that best fit your skills and travel plans, but don't limit yourself to just those. Try new things, maybe even treasure camping as discussed in a later chapter in this book.

You may find you like it or one of the other things covered, and chances are if you like whatever it is, you'll stick with it long enough to make money doing it.

With that said, it's time to start reading about all the income generating opportunities available to you.

Internet on the Road

As you view the different ways to make money in this book, you'll notice some require a reliable internet connection.

While some campgrounds do offer internet, most state and national parks and boondocking sites do not. Even in those parks where internet is available, it's usually unreliable, insecure, slow and difficult to connect to.

Fortunately, there is a solution to this problem. I cover it in the <u>Affordable High-Speed Internet</u> chapter at the end of this book. But before we get to that, let's cover some of the free ways to get internet while on the road.

Many restaurants and retailers offer free wi-fi for their customers. For example, McDonald's offers free internet access. You can stop in, grab a burger and hop online right inside their restaurant.

In some cases, you don't even have to go inside — you can pull up in their parking lot and log into their free internet while still in your vehicle. I've done it many times, and it usually works well.

Free internet is also often available at shopping centers and malls. Yes, they prefer you go inside hoping you'll shop and spend money at their stores. But in many cases, you can park outside the shopping center and log onto their free wi-fi. I've done it myself as I traveled around the country in my motorhome.

In addition to McDonald's and shopping centers, there are many places you can get free internet. Here are just a few of them:

Restaurants offering free Internet:

- Applebee's
- Arby's
- Burger King
- Chick-Fil-A
- Denny's
- Dunkin Donuts
- Einstein Bros.
- Jimmy John's
- Hooters
- IHOP
- Krispy Kreme
- Panera
- Quiznos
- Starbucks
- Subway
- Taco Bell
- Tim Horton's
- Wendy's

Retailers offering free Internet

- Apple Store
- Barnes & Noble
- Best Buy

4

- Lowes
- Macy's
- Michaels
- Meijer
- Nordstrom
- Office Depot
- Safeway
- Sam's Club
- Staples
- Target
- Whole Foods

Public Places with free internet

- Libraries
- Some public parks
- Some Government Buildings
- Some Town Squares

The above is a partial list, with more places adding free internet every day.

Free Wi-fi Finding App

An easy way to find free wi-fi while on the road is to use one of the free wi-fi finder apps for smartphones.

There are many available, including **WiFi Finder**, which is available for both Android and iPhones. WiFi Finder shows nearby free and public wi-fi networks with internet access.

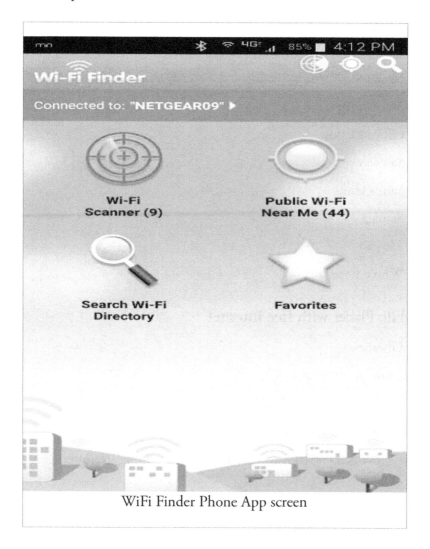

WiFi Finder Phone App screen

I've used WiFi Finder many times to help me find free internet connections, but I no longer need it as I now rely on the permanent wi-fi solution covered in the Affordable High-Speed

<u>Internet</u> chapter in this book.

Public WiFi Safety

Getting free internet from public networks is great, but there are potential problems. Browsing the internet and reading email over an open wifi network means information you send or receive over the network might be seen by others.

For that reason, follow these precautions:

- **Don't enter sensitive information** while on a public wi-fi network. Never enter your bank or credit card information or passwords on non-secured sites. Never include information in emails you wouldn't want others to gain access to.

- **Use 'https' (secure) websites** whenever possible. Facebook, Gmail, Amazon and other major sites will automatically use secure https when you connect. But many smaller sites won't. Avoid entering any personal information on those sites.

- **Unclick 'automatic connect'.** Unless you tell your mobile device otherwise, it will remember wi-fi networks you connect to and will try to automatically reconnect to those networks whenever you are in range. You may not even know your phone, tablet or computer has connected to the network, but hackers will. Avoid this potential problem by unchecking 'Connect Automatically' in your computer or phone's network settings.

The best solution to protecting your internet privacy is to avoid using public wi-fi. Instead, use your own dedicated private network like the one described in the <u>Affordable High-Speed Internet</u> chapter at the end of this book.

Work Camping

We're going to start off our search for income on the road with Work Camping (aka Workamping). Read on, and you'll understand why establishing yourself as a workamper can be an excellent foundation from which to launch many of the other income generating projects covered in this book.

With Work Camping, you agree to work at a campground or RV resort in exchange for a campsite with full hookups and use of all the campground facilities. Many work camping positions also pay an hourly wage.

Your job as a work camper could be as a host at a campground check-in station, a clerk at the camp store, a groundskeeper, campground maintenance or other campground related tasks.

Generally, when you apply for a workamper position, you'll know which job you are applying for. But often you'll be asked to do whatever needs to be taken care of at the campground. That sometimes includes cleaning the campground bathrooms.

As a workamper, you'll usually be expected to work at least twenty hours a week with a three-month commitment. On your time off, you'll be free to do whatever you want.

If you live full time in your RV and don't feel the need to continually move from one campground to another, being a workamper might be a good fit for you – especially if you find a position in a park that has the climate and/or amenities you enjoy.

Workamper positions are available at public and private RV parks across the country, from the Florida Keys to the northernmost parts of Alaska. This includes positions at many of the most spectacular parks in the country, places that normally have a long waiting list to get in as a paying guest.

As a workamper, you not only get to stay in the park for free, you often get paid to be there in exchange for a few hours of labor each week.

Because workampers have free time to pursue other interests, it can be an ideal job if you are writing a book, offering online services, or generating income using some of the other methods covered in this book.

If you do plan to become a workamper, be selective about the parks you choose. Be sure the climate, altitude, bugs and wildlife suit your lifestyle. And be sure the park and your campsite have the connections and amenities you need.

One way to check things out before taking on a Workamper position is to visit Workamping Reviews – a free website where you can read what others have to say about the parks they've worked in. Find the site at http://www.workampingreviews.com

Workamping job listing sites:

There are several websites that list work camper job openings. Here are some of the best:

- http://www.work-for-rvers-and-campers.com

- https://www.workamper.com

- http://workampingjobs.com

- http://www.rvparkstore.com/rv-park-help-wanted

- http://www.happyvagabonds.com/Jobs

- http://workatkoa.com/

- http://www.americanll.com/jobopenings

- http://hoodoorecreation.com/hoodoo-recreation-employment/

- http://www.workingcouples.com/

- http://www.camphost.org/

- http://www.rvnetwork.com/index.php?/forum/28-workers-wanted/

- http://www.camp-host.com

- https://www.volunteer.gov/

- http://cfaia.catsone.com/careers/

- https://careers.sunrvresorts.com/workcamper/

- http://www.rv-camping-lifestyle.com/workamper-jobs/

- http://roamingrv.com/rv-jobs/

- http://www.rvproperty.com/rv-job-listings/

- https://www.adventurelandpark.com/employment/work-camp/

- http://www.bluewaterkey.net/ (Key West!)

- http://www.snowbirdrvtrails.com/workkampingbystate.htm

- http://www.hillcountryrvresortnb.com/employment.php

- http://riversedgerv.co/work-exchange

- http://gastateparks.org/volunteer/hosts

- https://www.parks.ca.gov/?page_id=911

- https://www.blm.gov/wo/st/en/res/Volunteer.html

- http://www.jobmonkey.com/parks/

In addition to the above list, most public and private campgrounds offer workamper positions. If you are interested in a specific campground or location, visit their website to see if they list work opportunities. If they don't, give them a call and ask.

Keep in mind that experienced workampers usually move with the seasons and often book positions at choice parks several months in advance. If you are interested in a position at a top tier location in the high season, you'll want to apply early to avoid the rush.

Digital Nomad Jobs

If you consider yourself a digital nomad with computer or technical skills, you'll be happy to know there are many companies that hire off-site and remote personnel to provide professional services.

These companies are looking for:

- Programmers

- Developers

- IT managers

- Database managers

- Bookkeepers / Accountants / CPA's

- Lawyers

- Personal Assistants

- Web Designers

- Writers

- Editors

- Bloggers

- Podcasters

- Photographers

- Audio (voice over, audio books)

- Videographers

- Social Media Specialists
- Product Evangelists
- Graphic Designers
- Tutors
- Personal and Professional Coaches
- Consultants & Advisers
- Freelance Writers
- Transcriptionists
- Translators
- Researchers
- Content Creators
- Authors

Most of these positions allow you to set your own hours and choose the amount of work you want to commit to. Almost all pay well, and there are usually many open positions.

You can find listings for these jobs at these sites:

- **Working Nomads**
  https://www.workingnomads.co/jobs

- **Modern Day Nomads**
  http://www.moderndaynomads.com/

- **GitHub Remote Jobs List**
  https://github.com/jessicard/remote-jobs

- **Remote Working**
  http://www.remoteworking.co/

- **RemoteOK**
  https://remoteok.io/

- **Digital Nomad Job Finder**
  http://digitalnomad-jobfinder.com/

- **We Work Remotely**
  https://weworkremotely.com/

- **RemoteBase**
  https://remotebase.io/

- **FlexJobs**
  https://www.flexjobs.com/

- **FreeLancer**
  https://www.freelancer.com

- **UpWork**
  https://www.upwork.com/

- **PeoplePerHour**
  https://www.peopleperhour.com

In addition to the above, you can find a list of over 125 companies that hire 'virtual' staff to work remotely doing internet, graphics, and tech related jobs at
https://www.flexjobs.com/blog/post/virtual-companies-that-embrace-remote-working/

Caretaker Jobs

Property owners throughout the country often look for people to watch over their properties while they are away. These properties can include private homes, farms, ranches, forests and corporate locations.

In many cases, the preferred caretaker will be one who has a camper or RV and is willing to live on the property to watch over it. In most cases, the caretaker job will include an RV parking space with hookups and a small salary.

These kinds of jobs are ideal for singles or couples who prefer to avoid the socialization of RV parks and campgrounds and enjoy a bit of isolation.

Caretaker jobs can be found on the following websites.

- **Care Taker Jobs**
  http://www.caretaker-jobs.com

- **Working Couples**
  http://workingcouples.com/jobs-by-category/caretaker-couples-jobs

- **Caretaker Gazette**
  http://www.caretaker.org/

- **Estate Jobs**

http://www.jobboard.estatejobs.com/

- **Property Caretaker**
  https://www.indeed.com/q-Property-Caretaker-jobs.html

- **Ranch Work**
  http://www.ranchwork.com/

- **Craigslist**
  https://www.craigslist.org/about/sites
  search for 'caretaker' in the Jobs section

RV Dealer Transport Gigs

If you are over 25 and have a clean driving record and experience driving a motorhome or hauling a trailer, you might have the skills necessary to transport RVs, including fifth-wheels and camper trailers, from manufacturers to dealer locations.

Thousands of RVs are transported to dealers each month, and all require drivers or haulers to get them to their final destinations.

Most of these RV transporter jobs pay a dollar or more per mile driven – depending on the vehicle and the destination. Some will require specific licensing (e.g. CDL), but most won't.

 If you're the kind of person who likes to drive long distance and have a safe driving record, this kind of job might suit you.

Once approved by a transporter, you can pick and choose the jobs you want and avoid those that take you into areas where you are not comfortable driving. For example, you might want to avoid jobs that take you into New York City or Los Angeles due to the traffic congestion.

To find out more about RV transport jobs, check out the websites below.

* https://www.classictransport.com/

* http://www.synergyrvtransport.com/

* http://www.hoosier-rv-transport.com/drivers.htm

- http://www.rvtransportservice.com/driver

- http://www.bennettig.com/drive-for-bennett/rv-transportation-jobs/

- https://cwrvtransport.com/contractor/

- http://www.mapletreetransportation.com/

Roadie Delivery Driver Gigs

A new Uber-like service offers those who travel around the country in their RV or camper a chance to earn money delivering packages for individuals.

Here's how it works:

You visit the Roadie website and sign up as a driver. After signing up, you install the free Roadie app on your phone. When jobs become available, you bid on those that interest you.

The delivery jobs usually involve picking up and delivering packages across state lines. Typical items include paintings and other artwork, tools, family heirlooms, and even pets (if you sign up as a pet-friendly driver).

Your earnings as a Roadie driver will depend on the amount you bid to take on a delivery, whether your bids are accepted or not, and the frequency that you take on jobs.

At the time of this writing, Roadies Delivery is a new venture, and like many startups, its future is not assured.

But Roadie does offer an interesting opportunity for those who travel in an RV or camper and have room to carry items to be delivered to others.

To find out more about this service, visit https://www.roadie.com.

To sign up as a Roadie driver, visit https://www.roadie.com/roadies

Oil Field Gate Guard Jobs

If you don't mind living in your RV in remote areas with extreme climate conditions, you might be interested in a job as an oil gate guard. These jobs pay well, often $150 or more per day and don't require any strenuous labor.

The gate guard job involves manning the entry gate at oil fields and logging all vehicles that pass through. You'll be recording license plate numbers and the names of each person occupying vehicles that pass through the gate.

Most oil fields are in remote areas, with limited or no internet access, no neighbors, and no amenities. The drilling activities often generate a lot of noise, dust, and introduce oil fumes in the air.

As a gate guard, you cannot leave your position unless someone else is there to take your place. This means if you are single, you may need to have someone bring you supplies (food, water, etc.) as needed.

Being an oil gate guard is not a very glamorous position, but it pays well and might suit some people.

You can find oil gate guard openings on the following websites *(in some cases, you will have to call the number listed by the company name)*:

* http://oilgates.com

* http://gateguardservices.com

- http://swgateguards.com

- http://primogateguards.com/employment-opportunities/OverWatch

- **D&G Enterprises** (817)-291-2737 http://dandgenterprise.com/oil-field-security-companies

- **KC Services** (956)-236-5255

- **J&G Security** (512) 825-7567 http://oilgates.com/contact-us/

- **Loma Rentals LLC** http://www.lomarental.com/gate-guarding-and-site-supervision/

- **Pro Gate** (830)-776-8666

- **Trinity** (979)-241-1675

- **Oil Field Support Services** (361)-815-7050

- **Time Keepers** (956-821-5815)

- **Alcatraz Gate Guard Services** (817)-209-8602

Earning Money with YouTube Videos

Unless you've been living in a cave for the past ten years, you probably know that YouTube has become one of the most popular sites on the web.

What you may not know, is if you *monetize* your YouTube account, you can get paid by YouTube for every view the videos you post on YouTube get.

For example, one of my YouTube videos has over 800,000 views, and because I monetized it, YouTube has paid me several thousand dollars for those views. And that's for just one video.

Imagine what your earnings could be if you had hundreds of monetized videos on YouTube, and they were viewed by a lot of people. The income could be substantial.

Getting Started

So, you may be wondering, 'How does someone monetize a YouTube video?'

It's easy. All you need is a Gmail and YouTube account, and both are free.

To sign up for Gmail, go to www.gmail.com. To sign up for YouTube, go to www.youtube.com.

After you have both accounts, do this:

1. Log into your YouTube account

2. Go to the YouTube monetization page at https://www.youtube.com/account_monetization

3. Under the Monetization tab, click 'Enable My Account'

4. Accept the terms and conditions in the pop-up

5. A page will open with a 'Monetize' button. Click it.

6. After you have uploaded at least three videos and have views on those videos, go back to https://www.youtube.com/account_monetization

7. Find the 'How will I get paid' link and click on it.

8. Click on 'Associate an AdSense Account' link

9. On the next screen, submit your YouTube Channel

10. Click on "Continue"

11. Wait a couple of hours, and you should get an approval email

12. You can choose whether your earnings will be automatically deposited into your checking account or sent to you via mail.

After you receive your YouTube monetization approval email, you can go to your YouTube channel and if you've already uploaded videos, you can monetize each one.

To do this, select 'manage videos' and click the edit link beside each video. On the edit screen, click the 'Monetize' button to monetize the video.

When you upload new videos, you will be able to select the monetization feature on the upload screen.

Income Potential

YouTube says the income potential from monetized videos is unlimited. But the reality is, unless you upload a lot of videos or have one or more that go viral, you won't earn much money.

However, if you get into the habit of uploading one or two interesting videos a week and gain a YouTube following, it is possible to earn hundreds or even thousands of dollars a month from your monetized videos.

But don't expect immediate results. It usually takes time for your videos to be found, especially if you don't do anything to promote them or don't create videos on topics that people want to view. (*Find video topic ideas in upcoming chapters.*)

Like anything else, the more you work at it, the better your chances of success.

Start-up Costs

If you already have a camera or phone that can shoot video, a computer and internet access, there are no additional start-up costs. The only real costs will the time it takes to shoot (and edit) videos, and to upload them to YouTube.

Tools Needed

To earn income from the videos you post on YouTube, you will need a monetized YouTube account and videos you can upload.

To create videos, you'll want a camera that can record video. This can be a camcorder, a digital camera or smart phone.

You may also want a video editing program, but it's not required as you can use the online YouTube video editor. I use Vegas Movie Studio to edit my videos (Windows), but almost any video editing program will work. Not all videos need to be edited, but most do.

Pros

It costs nothing to get started. You can create and upload videos to YouTube from anywhere in the world as long as you have an internet connection. You can create videos on your schedule and on topics you find interesting. If one of your videos goes viral, you can quickly earn several thousand dollars.

Cons

There is no guarantee that any of your videos will gain any views or generate any income.

Tips for Success

- **Create short videos**, usually less than three minutes long. Viewers have short attention spans. Many tend to not click on videos that are longer.

- **Grab attention early in the video.** Give the viewer a reason to watch the rest of the video. Avoid boring the viewer, especially in the beginning of the video.

- **Keep the videos interesting**. Choose funny or weird subject matter. Things that people will want to share with others after they view.

- **Write an attention grabbing video title** when uploading to YouTube. Include words in the title that are related to the video subject matter, but also attract attention.

- **Write a compelling video description** that includes keywords and phrases that video viewers might be searching for.

- **Upload new videos often.** The more monetized videos you have on YouTube, the better the chance one or more will get a lot of views and pay off.

- **Avoid including copyrighted music** in your video audio track as these cannot be monetized and might be removed by YouTube.

- **Don't try to create Hollywood productions**. Just record things you find interesting and upload the videos to YouTube.

- See the **suggested video topic ideas** in the following chapters

Dash Cam Cash

As mentioned in the previous chapter, uploading monetized videos to YouTube can be quite lucrative – but only if you create and upload the kinds of videos people want to see.

Generally, the YouTube videos that get the most views, and earn their uploaders the most money, are those that:

- Are funny

- Entertaining

- Have cute cats, dogs, or other animals in them

- Are reviews of popular products

- Provide solutions to everyday problems

- Have wild or extreme weather

- Show road rage or accidents

- Are social media 'share worthy'

In you incorporate any of the above in your video topics, you'll usually get more views on YouTube. But there is no guarantee. Unfortunately, there is no surefire formula for creating a viral video, one that gets millions of views.

More often than not, videos that go viral are accidental creations. In most cases, someone was recording something else with their camera and accidentally captured something funny, awe inspiring or amazing.

A good example of this is dash cam videos. If you check YouTube, you'll find that many videos shot with dash cams have extremely high view counts.

In fact, a dash cam video that captured a meteor coming to earth got several million views, earning the person who uploaded it, thousands and thousands of dollars.

Dash cam videos that show people doing crazy things in traffic, weird roadside attractions, road rage and severe or unusual weather also get high view counts.

Because of this, if you want to earn money with YouTube videos, I strongly recommend you get a dash cam and set it to automatically record video every time your drive your RV or camper.

Doing this will help you capture footage of anything interesting or unusual you see while on the road.

If you've spent much time on the road, you've undoubtedly seen things that if captured on video, would have drawn an audience on YouTube. If the video had been monetized, it could be earning you money.

Having a dash cam to capture the weirdness on the road can quickly pay for itself when you upload videos from it to YouTube.

Income Potential

As mentioned in a previous chapter, monetized videos on YouTube can earn pennies or tens of thousands of dollars. It all depends on how many videos you upload and how many people view them.

Some well-known RV'ers upload videos at least once a week and are able to cover their on-the-road living expenses from their YouTube earnings. Not all will be able to cover their expenses by uploading YouTube videos, but many road warriors are.

When it comes to how much you can earn, in 2016 the number one independent YouTuber is reported to have earned twelve million dollars from his monetized videos (they were not RV related).

Start-up Costs

When it comes to recording dash cam videos, your start-up costs will include the price of a good quality dash cam and a micro SD memory card. You can get both for under one hundred dollars. See suggested models below.

Tools Needed

To record dash cam videos, you'll need a decent dash cam and a way to mount it to your windshield. While it is possible to use a hand-held cell phone to record videos, it is dangerous to do so while driving, and it may not catch the spontaneous events that occur unexpectedly while on the road.

For that reason, I prefer a dedicated dash cam, wired to start recording as soon as I start my vehicle. The two dash cams I recommend are:

- **G1WC** - available at Amazon for around $50. Includes a windshield and mirror mount and power cable. Add a 32 gbyte micro SD card (about $14 on Amazon). This budget dash cam records better than average video quality and is affordable.

- **Viofo A119** - for higher quality video, get this one. Available on Amazon and eBay for around $80, includes everything you need to get started, except for the 64 gbyte micro SD card. This is the one I now have.

Both of the above dash cams are easy to install, have interval recording and automatic video locking in the event of an accident. Both record in standard mp4 format, with date and time-stamped video clips.

Because dash cams are continually improving, you may want to visit https://dashcamtalk.com/ to find the latest recommended cameras.

Getting Started

Getting started with dash cam video is easy. Just buy and install a dash cam in your vehicle.

Installation is simple. Just mount the dash cam on your windshield using the included suction mount and plug the included power cable into a 12-volt power receptacle (aka cigarette lighter).

When you drive, the dash cam will record everything in front of your vehicle. If during your travels, you see a YouTube worthy event, note the time of day. When you park, download the video from the dash cam's SD card to your computer and then upload to YouTube.

Pros

Recording dash cam video is easy and automatic. Should your dash cam record something noteworthy, it costs nothing to upload the footage to YouTube. If you drive in interesting areas or weather conditions, you'll probably end up with video clips worthy of uploading to YouTube.

If you are in an accident and the other driver is at fault, your dash cam video can provide proof of your innocence.

Cons

You'll have to spend at least $50 to buy a decent dash cam and you'll have to install it in your vehicle. If you don't travel much, it won't record much.

Tips for Success

- Make sure your dash cam is mounted so that it gets a clear, level and wide angle view of the road ahead.

- Make sure your dash cam starts recording automatically when you start your vehicle. This option is built into most dash cams.

- Keep your windshield clean so the dash cam can get a clear image.

- Adjust the dash cam as needed to make sure your windshield's sunshades haven't knocked it off kilter.

- By default, your dash cam records audio unless you turn it off in settings. This means it records conversations, as well as anything else heard inside your vehicle. If uploading video to YouTube, you'll probably want to mute the audio for privacy reasons.

- If you record an interesting event, use the 'lock file' button on the dash cam to prevent overwriting that part of the video until you have time to download it.

- Set your dash cam to record in 1080p 30fps for higher quality video.

- If uploading to YouTube, use a video editing program to delete the boring parts of the video so that the interesting part starts within ten seconds.

Product Review Video Income

Posting product review videos on YouTube is another way to generate income. These can get lots of views, and on a monetized YouTube account can generate a nice income.

Living in an RV or camping van, you can shoot video reviews of products you use while camping or on the road.

Reviewed products can include GPS systems, phones, seat cushions, camping gear, kitchen appliances, cables, hoses, windshield covers, storage solutions and any other accessories you use on the road.

You can also create campground review videos with a drive through of the campground (recorded on your dash cam), and a review of the campground facilities. You can also record video reviews of nearby attractions and events.

If you search YouTube for RV related videos, you'll find thousands, many with hundreds of thousands of views.

For example, a recent video showing how to stay warm in an RV got more than 300,000 views in just a few days. If the video had been monetized, it would have earned the person who posted it more than a thousand dollars the first month it was online.

If you look around your RV or camper, you'll probably find many worthy topics that would fit within a short three-minute video.

Income Potential

As mentioned in a previous chapter, monetized videos on YouTube can earn pennies or tens of thousands of dollars. It all depends on whether the video is monetized and how many people view it.

The more monetized videos you have on YouTube, the better your chances of generating income from them. Some RV'ers earn enough from their YouTube videos to cover all their living expenses.

Start-up Costs

To create product review videos, you'll need a camera or phone that can record video as well as audio. You'll also want a computer and video editing program.

Total start-up costs, assuming you already own a computer and a phone or camera that can record video, could be close to zero. If you need to purchase a camera to record video, start-up costs will be higher. Cameras that can record decent video cost fifty dollars and up. You may also want an inexpensive lavalier microphone (if the camera has an audio input port), to get clearer voice recordings.

Tools Needed

As mentioned above, to record videos, you'll need a camera or phone that can record video. To get better audio, you'll probably want a lavalier microphone – if your camera has a microphone port. Most smartphones have this capability, as well as some video and photo cameras.

If you're starting out with no way to record video, here's a list of tools you'll need:

- Camera or phone that can record video ($50 and up)

- Lavalier or external microphone ($20 and up)

- Computer ($200 and up)

- Video Editing Software (free or up to $100)

I usually record my videos with a Canon pocket photo camera and edit them with Vegas Movie Studio Platinum v12 (under $50).

Pros

If you like to talk about products you use or places you visit, recording review videos might come naturally to you. It costs nothing but time to record and edit the videos, and if they are well liked on YouTube, you can create a following and a steady income.

Cons

If you are uncomfortable appearing on camera or speaking about products or places you visit, you probably will not enjoy creating product review videos. It can be a struggle if words don't come naturally while you're showing or talking about a product.

Tips for Success

- **Keep the videos short** (three minutes or less) and on point. Avoid rambling and straying off topic.

- **Make sure the audio is easy to listen to** at a pleasant volume with no distracting hums, buzzes or background noises.

- **Avoid camera zooms and too much camera motion.** Don't

make your viewers seasick.

- **Put your camera on a tripod** and only appear in the video when necessary. People usually want to see what you are reviewing, not you.

- **Be upbeat and happy when on video.** It's contagious, and your viewers will appreciate feeling good after viewing your videos

- **No curse words, no negativity**.

- **Edit ruthlessly.** Delete sections of video that are boring or irrelevant. Keep the videos short and interesting, or viewers will simply click away.

- Use **still photos to show closeups** and detail.

- Get better at creating video by shooting and editing videos regularly.

- **Give viewers a reason to subscribe to your YouTube channel.** More subscribers mean more people will learn about and view, videos you upload.

- **View tips on creating and editing videos on YouTube**, including my own channel, https://www.youtube.com/guerillabill

Get Paid to Write Books

There's never been a better time to write and publish books than right now. These days, you no longer need to find a publisher and beg them to publish your book. Nor do you need to pay a printing company setup fees and buy a required number of copies to get your book in print.

If you write a book, you can use free services from Amazon to get your book published online for zero out of pocket costs. Amazon will promote your book, take orders for it, collect payments and deliver your book to buyers – and at the end of each month, Amazon will send you a payment for your book royalties.

Even better, you can use Amazon's CreateSpace print-on-demand service to make your book available in print as well as in Kindle format. Again, with zero out of pocket costs.

Amazon pays up to 70% royalties on your book sales – far better than any of the major publishing companies pay. This means earnings from your book sales can add up quickly, especially if you write and publish several books.

But what if you've never written a book? How do you get started and what should you write about?

Getting Started

Getting started writing books is fairly easy. You'll need a computer with a keyboard and a word processing program. I use a Windows notebook computer and the free LibreOffice Writer program, which is a Microsoft Word clone.

When I start a new book, I download and open the free Kindle Book template, found on my website at http://www.bmyers.com. This template is available for Word, OpenOffice Writer, and LibreOffice Writer. It opens as a perfectly formatted ready-to-write book. Everything you need is in it, all you have to do is write.

And yes, the template is free, no strings attached.

With the book template, you enter your book title, your author name, chapter title and start writing.

What to write about?

The big question is, 'what should your book be about?'

The answer – anything you want.

For example, you could write a 'list' book. Something like '30 things to know before going full time in your RV' or '18 ways to improve your life' or '10 steps to financial independence' or '15 foods you should never eat if you want to lose weight'.

These 'list' books are fairly easy to write, assuming you choose a topic you know about. With today's short attention span internet buyers, list books do quite well on Amazon.

Or, you could write a children's book. These are often thirty-six pages or less, have fewer than forty words per page, and are usually about a wayward duck, goat, pig or some other animal. Most are illustrated.

Children's books can be fun to write, and if you can draw, they can be fun to illustrate.

Or you could write a how-to book about a skill or hobby. I've written a few of these myself, including, 'How to buy a used RV without getting burned', and 'Convert your Mini-van into a Mini-RV camper.'

Other books you could create include coloring books, cookbooks, travel books, joke books, biographies and short stories and fiction novels.

Income Potential

When you publish your book on Amazon, you can earn up to a 70% royalty. Most Kindle eBooks are priced at $2.99 and up, which means you'll earn $2.05 per sale. Printed copies sell for $12.95 and up, with an average $3.00 profit per book.

If Amazon sells five hundred copies of your $2.99 eBook, they'll pay you a thousand dollars. If they sell a thousand copies, they'll pay you two thousand dollars.

To earn more each month, write more books. The more you have for sale, the more you'll earn each month.

Start-up Costs

Assuming you already have a computer, you don't need much else to get started writing a book. You will need a Word compatible word processing program. I recommend either OpenOffice Writer or LibreOffice Writer. Both are Word clones, and both are free. Find them at:

- http://www.openoffice.org

- https://www.libreoffice.org

Before you publish your book, you'll want to have a professional cover created (unless you know how to do it yourself). You can get custom book covers created for forty dollars or less at http://www.goonwrite.com

Tools Needed

As mentioned above, to get started writing your book, you'll need a computer, preferably one with a full-size keyboard and a word processing program. If you plan to include photos in your book, you'll need a digital camera.

You'll also need an account at Amazon.com, and you'll need to join their free Kindle Direct Publishing Program at https://kdp.amazon.com.

Pros

As a published Amazon author, you will earn income from your book sales without the hassles of taking orders, processing credit cards or stocking book inventory. You can write on your own schedule, choose book topics that appeal to you and write from anywhere in the world.

There is no limit to the number of books you can publish on Amazon. You'll earn income from each book, and often the income will continue for years.

Cons

Writing a book takes time and dedication. You'll need a place where you can set up your computer and write undisturbed. It's extremely easy to lose motivation and never finish the book.

Unpublished books will earn you zero money.

Tips for Success

- **Don't try to write the next great American novel.** Instead, choose a topic you are familiar with, and write a how-to or tip book about it. You can write the novel later.

- **Simplify your writing** by starting out with a template. Find my free Kindle Book Template at https://www.bmyers.com/public/Kindle-Nonfiction-template.cfm

- **Set a goal of writing a certain number of pages or words per day.** When I write, my goal is ten pages a day. If I can keep that up, after twenty days, I'll have a two-hundred-page book.

- **Use photographs and illustrations to help readers visualize what you are writing about.** In my 'Convert Your Mini Van to a Mini RV, I used more than sixty photos.

- **Search Amazon best-selling nonfiction for book ideas.** When searching Amazon for book ideas, use these keywords, "secrets", "facts", "little known", "steps", "easy", "tips", "tricks", "basic", "things", "rules", "reasons", "ways".

- **Don't overprice your book.** Doing so reduces sales and profits and increases reader expectations. Keeping the Kindle price between $2.99 and $3.99 will generate more sales and fewer complaints. Keep the price of the printed versions of your book under $15.00.

- **Consider using a book editing service to proofread your**

book. Find book editors at http://www.fiverr.com

- **Don't over think the publishing process.** Once the book is completed, save the file as a MS Word Doc, and upload to your Amazon KDP account. Amazon will do the rest.

- **Create a print version.** After the Kindle version of the book is created, use www.createspace.com to have it converted to print.

- **Find help online.** If you have questions about formatting or publishing your book, search YouTube and Amazon KDP for answers. Also, search my site (http://www.bmyers.com), and you'll find videos showing each step of the book publishing process.

- **Don't be afraid no one will like what you write.** It might surprise you how many people will appreciate the words you put on the page.

- **Worth repeating – keep it simple.** Choose a topic or book genre that you feel comfortable writing about. Maybe a children's book about traveling the US in a motorhome. Or a book where your favorite pet is the lead character. Or a book about how to find affordable snowbird locations in the south.

- **Choose a book topic that is easy and enjoyable** for you to write about.

- **Don't get discouraged and quit**. All writers are insecure about their work. You just have to learn to power through.

Writing Children's Books

One of last year's best-selling children's books had fewer than forty pages with less than twenty words per page. The book sold more than a half-million copies and spawned a series of similar books from the same author.

In published interviews, the author said he wrote the first book over a weekend, just scribbling down funny words he thought his child would enjoy. Below the words, he drew a funny doodle. He did this on thirty-two pages and printed out a copy which he gave to his child.

After seeing how much his own child enjoyed the book, he decided to publish it for others. Income from his now expanded series has been reported to be well over a million dollars a year.

If doing something like this appeals to you, you might be the right person to create your own line of children's books.

As mentioned in the previous chapter, writing and getting a book published has never been easier. You no longer have to find a publisher and beg them to publish your book. Nor do you have to pay a printing company setup fees and buy a hundred copies to get your book in print.

These days, you can use free services from Amazon to get your book published and promoted for zero out of pocket costs. Amazon will do all the work for you, including creating a sales page, taking orders, collecting payments and delivering the book to buyers.

They'll even get the book printed for you. At the end of each month, Amazon will send you a check or direct deposit to your bank.

Amazon pays up to 70% royalties on your book sales – far better than any of the major publishing companies pay. This means earnings from your book sales can add up quickly, especially if you write and publish several books.

But what if you've never written a children's book? How do you get started and what should you write about?

Getting Started

Getting started writing children's books is fairly easy. One of the best ways is to visit 'free books of the day' sites like http://www.ereaderiq.com/freebies?c=155009011.

There you'll find hundreds of free books, including a selection of children's books. Download some of these, and you're almost certain to find inspiration for your own book.

As you review children's books written by others, you'll see that most are thirty-six pages or less and include a few words at the top of the page followed by an illustration that fills the rest of the page.

To create a book in this format, you'll need a computer, an occasional internet connection, and a word processing program. I use a Windows computer and the free LibreOffice Writer program which is a MS Word clone that works on Windows as well as Mac.

If you have MS Word, use it. Or if you prefer, use the free LibreOffice Writer or OpenOffice Writer.

Find them at:

- http://www.openoffice.org
- https://www.libreoffice.org

Before you publish your book, you'll want to have a professional cover created (unless you know how to do it yourself). You can get a custom book cover created for forty dollars or less at http://www.goonwrite.com

You'll also need a source of illustrations for your children's book. You can either create your own using a drawing program, free clip art or public domain images. You can even use photos you shoot or illustrations you draw and scan onto your computer.

You can also find affordable children's book illustrators at https://www.fiverr.com (search for children's book illustrator).

Starting a new book

When I start a new book, I download and open the free Kindle Book non fiction template found on my website at http://www.bmyers.com. This template is available for MS Word, OpenOffice Writer, and LibreOffice Writer and opens as a ready-to-write book, formatted for publishing at Amazon.

Everything you need is in the template, and all you have to do is write. And yes, the template is free, no strings attached.

Most illustrated children's books have a simple story, usually about an animal trying to overcome a hardship or learning a life lesson. You can probably come up with a story based on your own experiences with children or grandchildren, using a pet or other animal or insect as the hero of the tale.

Write a first draft, not worrying too much about punctuation, spelling or illustrations. Get it completed, then go back and edit and add illustrations. Then upload to Amazon to be published.

Income Potential

When you publish your books on Amazon, you'll earn a 70% royalty. Most Kindle eBooks are priced at $2.99 and up, which means you'll earn at least $2.05 per sale. Printed copies sell for $12.95 and up, with an average $3.00 profit per book.

If Amazon sells five hundred copies of your $2.99 eBook each month, they'll pay you a thousand dollars. If they sell a thousand copies, you'll earn two thousand dollars.

To increase your monthly book royalties, write more book. The more books you have for sale, the more you are likely to earn each month.

Keep in mind that book sales at Amazon are not automatic, at least in the beginning. You'll do better by promoting your book in some way, whether it's to friends and family, on social media, or through some of the book review sites available online.

Start-up Costs

Assuming you already have a computer, you'll need only an MS Word compatible word processing program. I recommend either OpenOffice Writer or LibreOffice Writer. Both are Word clones, and both are free.

You'll want to invest in having a professional cover created for your book (unless you know how to do it yourself). You can get a custom book cover created for forty dollars or less at http://www.goonwrite.com.

For children's book illustrations, you can create them yourself, use free clip art or public domain art, or find an illustrator at http://www.fiverr.com to create them for you.

These custom images from Fiverr start at five dollars each and go up. If you have a thirty-six-page book and need thirty-six images, it might cost you under two hundred dollars to have your book illustrated.

Total start-up costs (assuming you own a computer) could be zero. The costs will go up if you need to pay an illustrator, but still should be quite affordable.

Tools Needed

As mentioned above, to get started writing your book, you will need a computer, preferably one with a full-size keyboard and a word processing program. I use LibreOffice Writer, an MS Word clone.

You'll also need an account at Amazon.com, and you'll need to join their free Kindle Direct Publishing Program at https://kdp.amazon.com

Pros

As a published Amazon author, you will earn income from your book sales without the hassles of taking orders, processing credit cards or stocking book inventory. You can write your book on your own schedule, choose a story line that appeals to you, and write from anywhere in the world.

There is no limit to the number of books you can publish at Amazon. You'll earn income from each book, and often the income will continue for years.

Cons

You'll need a place where you can set up your computer and write undisturbed. It's easy to lose motivation and never finish the book. Unpublished books will not earn you any money.

Tips for Success

- **Start by reviewing successful children's books** sold on Amazon. Use them as a guide or template when it comes to story format and page layout.

- **Simplify your writing by starting out with a template.** Find my free Kindle Book Template at https://www.bmyers.com/public/Kindle-Nonfiction-template.cfm

- **Set a goal of writing a certain number of pages or words per day.** When I write, my goal is ten pages a day. If I can keep that up, after twenty days, I'll have a two-hundred-page book. With a children's book, you won't need that many pages.

- **Use photographs and illustrations to help the reader to visualize what you are writing about.** In my 'Convert Your Mini Van to a Mini RV, I used more than sixty photos.

- **Don't overprice your book.** Doing so reduces sales and profits and increases reader expectations. Keeping the price between $2.99 and $3.99 will generate more sales and fewer complaints.

- **Consider using a book editing service** to proofread your book.

Find editors at http://www.fiverr.com (search for book editor)

- **When writing a children's book, keep it fun and interesting.** Imagine being a parent and reading the book with the child. Make it fun for both.

- **Read your book out loud,** just as a parent might do with a child. Hear what the words sound like. If you stumble over words, change them. Make it easy for both parent and child to read and follow along.

- **Don't over think the publishing process.** Once the book is completed, save the file in MS Word Doc format, and upload it to your Amazon KDP account. Amazon will do the rest.

- **Use an attention-grabbing cover** as well as a book title that will interest parents as well as children.

- When you enter the book at Amazon, **include keywords that describe the book as 'fun', 'entertaining' and other things a parent might search for** in the children's book category.

- After the Kindle version of the book is created, use www.createspace.com, to have it **converted to print.**

- **Don't be afraid no one will like your book.** Some of the best-selling children's books are the goofiest. It might surprise you how many people will appreciate the words you put on the page.

- **With children's books, illustrations are important.** Choose ones that are fun to look at and include color.

- **Don't get discouraged and quit.** All writers are insecure about their work. You just have to learn to power through.

Finding Paying Gigs on Fiverr

If you have internet access and a computer, you have all you need to start finding paying gigs on the https://www.fiverr.com/ website.

On the Fiverr site, you post a free listing offering services you can provide, and visitors to the site will contact you with the small projects they want you to bid on.

In most cases, the jobs will be related to graphic design, marketing, writing, editing, photography, website creation or maintenance, music creation, programming, voice over, and illustrations.

For example, under the graphic design gigs, you could offer to create:

- Company Logos
- Business Cards & Stationery
- Cartoons & Caricatures
- Flyers & Posters
- Book Covers
- Banner Ads
- 3D & 2D Models
- T-Shirts
- Infographics
- Clip Art

- Invitations

Each of the above would be a separate gig. So, if you felt comfortable creating Company Logos, you'd post a listing on Fiverr offering to create logos.

In the listing, you'd include examples of what you can do and the base price you charge along with add-on prices for extras.

When someone needing a company logo sees your listing, they contact you through the Fiverr service. They tell you what they want to create for them, and after reviewing their request, you reply with a price you'll charge to do the work.

If they agree to your price, they submit a payment to Fiverr to cover your fee (through PayPal). When the work is completed and delivered, Fiverr releases the payment to you.

Graphics & Design   Digital Marketing   Writing & Translation   Video & Animation   Music & Audio   Programming & Tech   Advertising   More

How It Works

1. Create A Gig

Sign up for free, set up your Gig, and offer your work to our global audience.

2. Deliver Great Work

Get notified when you get an order and use our system to discuss details with customers.

3. Get Paid

Get paid on time, every time. Payment is transferred to you upon order completion.

Signing up with Fiverr is free, whether as a customer or service provider. You can list as many services as you like.

Frequently asked questions about Fiverr

Q. What can you sell?

A. You can offer any service you wish as long it's legal and complies with Fiverr's terms. There are over 100 categories you can browse to get ideas.

Q. How much money can you make?

A. It's totally up to you. You can work as much as you want. Many sellers work on Fiverr full time and some keep their 9-5 job while using Fiverr to make extra money.

Q. How much does it cost?

A. It's free to join Fiverr. There is no subscription required or fees to list your services. You keep 80% of each transaction.

Q. How much time will I need to invest?

A. It's very flexible. You need to put in some time and effort in the beginning to learn the marketplace and then you can decide for yourself what amount of work you want to do.

Q. How do I price my service?

A. With Gig Packages, you set your pricing anywhere from $5 - $995 and offer three versions of your service at three different prices.

Q. How do I get paid?

A. Once you complete a buyer's order, the money is transferred to your account. No need to chase clients for payments and wait 60 or 90 days for a check.

How to decide if Fiverr is for you

If you have almost any skill, whether it be a technical computer skill or a non-technical skill like doing celebrity impersonations or voice overs, you'll find opportunities on Fiverr.

But if you don't have a computer or an internet connection and aren't able to devote a little time to post your gigs on Fiverr.com, it won't be something you'll want to do.

That said, be sure to review the opportunities I cover in the next few chapters. What you see might change your mind.

Voice Over & Narration Gigs

If you have an interesting speaking voice, you might be able to find paying gigs doing voice over and narration work. These jobs can be as simple as reading thirty seconds' worth of text or narrating a full-length novel.

Income will depend on the scope of the job and the amount of text to be read. Most gigs start at five dollars per one hundred words. Prices will go higher for more words or for special requests.

Income Potential

If you can attract a steady flow of clients seeking voice over work, you could conceivably earn several hundred dollars a month doing narrations for YouTube videos, voice mail, and radio and TV commercials.

If you sign up as a voice narrator in Amazon's ACX program, you can earn one hundred dollars an hour or more, narrating books.

As you gain experience, you can expand your offerings to include voice work for movie trailers, documentaries, business presentations, animated characters and more.

Start-up Costs

The biggest expense when getting into voice narration is the purchase of a high-quality microphone. If recording direct to your computer (as many people do), you'll need a microphone that can be connected via USB (assuming your computer has a USB port), and you'll need audio recording software.

For software, you can use the free Audacity program. It has all the features you need and includes filters and plug-ins that can enhance your voice and remove unwanted noise.

For a microphone, expect to pay a hundred dollars or more for a cardioid condenser microphone with a pop filter. You may also need an analog to USB converter so you can connect the microphone to your computer.

To keep out background noise, you may need to build a simple 'cone of silence' box around the microphone. You'll find plenty of videos on YouTube showing how.

Tools Needed

As mentioned above, you'll need a computer, a microphone with pop filter and noise cancellation, and an audio capture and editing program.

When it comes to computers, either a Mac or Windows will do. The computer should have a USB port and enough room on the hard drive to store audio files (most will be under 20 mbytes).

For audio editing, I recommend starting with the free Audacity program. You'll find many videos on the web showing how to use it to enhance your vocal recordings, including my own YouTube video, 'Enhance voice in audio and video recordings with Audacity'.

When it comes to microphones, prices for quality units start at $100 and go up quickly. A good lower budget USB microphone is the Blue Yeti Blackout Edition. It's available on Amazon for around

$100. If you get that microphone be sure to order the pop filter – it's an additional eight dollars.

Many pros recommend the Rode NT1-A Cardioid Condenser Microphone Recording Package with a Tripod Base which is available on Amazon for around $240. It uses an XLR connection, which means if you want to connect to your computer, you'll need an XLR to USB interface. These start at around $100.

You may want to invest in a set of headphones so you can listen to recordings while recording and editing. Expect to pay around $60 for a decent set.

A good entry level recording system with microphone, stand, headphones and audio recording software can be put together for under $200.

Getting Started

The quickest way to get started in the voice narration business is to sign up for an account at http://www.fiverr.com and post an ad offering voice over and narration work.

Before writing your ad, review ads posted by others offering narration services and use those as a guide for your own ad.

Set your prices near what others are asking and be sure to include two examples of your narration and voice over work on your Fiverr page.

After you have developed a portfolio of your voice over work, you might want to sign up with the Amazon ACX program.

Find details at http://www.acx.com/help/narrators/200484550.

You can also find voice over gigs listed on the web at many job sites including:

- https://www.voices.com/jobs

- https://voice123.com/

- https://www.thevoicerealm.com/voice-over-jobs-online.php

- http://www.edgestudio.com/voice-over-jobs

Pros

If you have an interesting speaking voice, offering voice overs and narrations can be a good way to earn extra spending money. You can charge the prices you want, choose the jobs you like, work on your own schedule, and record from anywhere in the world.

Cons

If you don't have a suitable speaking voice, you won't do well as a voice over or narration pro. If you park your RV in a place with a lot of loud background noise (construction, traffic, airplanes, etc.), it'll be difficult to record quality narration unless you build a sound booth. The cost of recording equipment, even at the two-hundred-dollar level, may be more than some will want to spend.

There is a lot of competition for the higher paying jobs, especially those in movies and broadcast TV.

Tips for Success

- Review the most successful voice over ads at Fiverr and use those as a guide to creating your own ad.

- Include voice-over and narration sample audio clips in your ad postings at http://www.fiverr.com.

- Offer several voice over packages with prices to reflect the number of words to be read and the time frame the product needs to be delivered.

- Offer to do voice-overs for radio and TV commercials, movies, YouTube videos, short stories and if you are up to it, full-length book narration.

- Check your email every few hours to make sure you don't miss client project requests from Fiverr.

- Ask your clients to reward your work with five-star reviews.

- Only take on jobs you feel qualified to work on; turn down those that don't fit your requirements.

- Use professional microphones and deliver high-quality work. Don't disappoint customers with shoddy quality.

- Provide quick turn-around to keep your clients happy.

- Sign up at several freelance sites where you can find voice over gigs as well as post information about the services you offer.

- Check the local Craigslist for voice-over and narration gigs.

Income from Jingles & Drops

If you find yourself making up words to songs or creating new tunes on a keyboard, you might be the right person to start earning income by creating Jingles and Drops.

You probably already know what jingles are – they are the short musical tracks used on radio that brand a product. You can probably think of a few, but if not, remember the Oscar Meyer Wiener jingle?

It's simple but catchy, and someone got paid quite a bit to come up with it.

If that sounds like something you could do, then it's a service you can offer on Fiverr.

Even if you can't sing, you can create Drops – short phrases or musical clips, including sound effects, used during radio commercials and programs to add interest or wake up listeners.

Believe it or not, there's a pretty good market for both, and it's easy to get started.

You will need a computer and the ability to record the jingles or drops you create. In most cases, you'll want to use an audio editing program that has easy-to-use built-in special effects. These can enhance your drop or jingle and make it sound like you are working in a studio instead of the back of your camper.

To get an idea of the kind of Jingles and Drops being offered on

Fiverr, check out https://www.fiverr.com/categories/music-audio/jingles-drops

Income Potential

The amount of money you can earn creating Jingles and Drops depends on the volume of work you do, the fees you charge your clients and the extras that you include with each job (like commercial ownership rights).

Small jobs will pay thirty to forty dollars while larger jobs, especially for major corporate clients, will pay more.

If you are able to satisfy your customers, you may find a steady stream of work, especially from radio stations and podcast bloggers.

Start-up Costs

At a minimum, you will need a computer with audio editing software and an internet connection. You'll probably want a microphone as well headphones. You may also want a musical instrument (keyboard, guitar, ukulele, kazoo, etc.).

Depending on what you already have, your start-up costs could range from zero to hundreds of dollars.

Tools Needed

At the very least, you'll need a computer with internet connection, an audio editing program, a microphone, and headphones. You'll also need a free account at Fiverr.com

Starting out, you can use the free Audacity audio-editing program and the many free sound effects plug-ins available for it. You can find Audacity at http://www.audacityteam.org/.

Getting Started

The quickest way to get started as a jingle and drop provider is to sign up for an account at http://www.fiverr.com and post an ad offering to create Jingles and another one for Drops.

Before writing your ads, review ads posted by others offering these services and use those a guide for your own.

Set your prices near what others are asking and be sure to include examples of at least one of your creations on your Fiverr page.

Pros

If you have a knack for coming up with funny or memorable jingles, offering to create them for others can be a good way to earn extra spending money. You can charge the prices you want, choose the jobs you like, work on your own schedule and from anywhere in the world.

Cons

If you have a tin ear and aren't able to come up with a funny jingle, this won't be for you.

Also note that there is a lot of competition for the higher paying jobs, especially those for large corporate clients.

Tips for Success

- Review the most successful jingle and drop ads at Fiverr and use those as a guide to creating your own.

- Include a memorable jingle or drop audio clip in your ad postings at http://www.fiverr.com

- Offer several packages with prices to reflect the length of the audio file and the number of words in the jingle and the time frame the product needs to be delivered.

- Offer to do jingles and drops for radio and TV commercials, YouTube videos, web pages, and podcasts.

- Check your email every few hours to make sure you don't miss client project requests from Fiverr.

- Ask your clients to reward your work with five-star reviews.

- Only take on jobs you feel qualified to work on. Turn down those that don't fit your schedule.

- Strive to deliver high-quality work. Don't disappoint customers with shoddy quality.

- Provide quick turn-around to keep your clients happy.

- Check local Craigslist for jingle creation gigs.

Flyers & Posters for Profit

Almost every business, event, and attraction needs a flyer or poster at some point. These promotional items are used to attract new customers or announce new services or upcoming events.

Because so many business and event sponsors need these, there is a strong and ongoing demand for them. If you have graphic skills or have access to the poster and flyer creation tools and resources I mention later in this chapter, you could generate income by offering flyers and poster creation services on sites like Fiverr.

Here's an example of how it could work.

A small-time music promoter is planning a future event, and he visits the Fiverr website in search of someone to create an event poster. He searches for 'event poster' and looks through the examples that Fiverr creators have posted. He finds one he likes (yours), and asks you to submit a bid price to create one for his event.

He agrees to your price, and you create the poster. After he approves your work, you get paid, and you deliver a digital file of the poster, which the promoter can take to a local printer to have printed.

If he likes your work, he may provide you a steady stream of work creating posters and flyers for upcoming events. Others who see your work may do the same.

Creating Posters and Flyers

Creating posters, flyers, and brochures while on the road can be fairly easy – if you have a computer, graphic software and a library of pre-made templates for posters, brochures and flyers.

The advantage of creating posters and flyers using your computer is you don't have to worry about needing large areas to work in or paint brushes or drawing tools. It can all be done on your computer, and when completed, you can upload the finished image file to your client.

Income Potential

Many creators on Fiverr advertise to create custom posters, brochures, and flyers with a starting price of five dollars. But if you look closer, the starting price quickly escalates, and the typical charge for a completed project will be fifty dollars or more.

If you structure your fees similarly, you can expect to net at least forty-five dollars per project. While that doesn't sound like much money, prices will go up depending on the work involved and variables like number of pages (for flyers and brochures).

Startup Costs

Getting starting as a poster and flyer creator at Fiverr.com won't cost you anything. It is free to post an ad on Fiverr offering your services.

If you don't already have a computer and some graphic software and the skill to use both, this probably isn't the right opportunity for you.

Tools Needed

To create posters, flyers, and brochures, you'll need a computer, an occasional internet connection, a PayPal account (to receive payment), and an account at www.fiverr.com.

Most people who create posters, flyers, and brochures start with ready-made templates that they can quickly customize.

You can find templates for posters, flyers, brochures and more at:

- https://www.canva.com/
- https://www.postermywall.com/
- https://www.posterini.com/
- http://www.ronyasoft.com/products/poster-forge/
- https://www.lucidpress.com/pages/templates
- http://www.brother.com/creativecenter
- https://templates.office.com/en-us/Brochures
- https://templates.office.com/en-us/Flyers
- https://www.smiletemplates.com
- http://www.stocklayouts.com/
- https://www.smiletemplates.com/
- http://www.pixeden.com/brochure-templates
- http://www.freepik.com/free-photos-vectors/poster-template

Pros

If you already have a computer and graphic design skills, creating custom posters, flyers and brochures via Fiverr can make good use of your skills and reward you with extra spending money.

Cons

If you don't enjoy working on a computer or learning to use new tools and software, or if it takes you more than a few hours to create a custom poster or flyer, this business won't be for you.

Tips for Success

- Review the most successful poster and flyer creation ads at Fiverr and use those as a guide to creating your own ad.

- Include several examples of poster or flyer mockups in your ad

- Offer several packages with prices to reflect the variety of work you offer and the time frame in which they can be delivered.

- Offer a make-over service for clients, using their existing flyers and brochures as a starting point.

- Check your email every few hours to make sure you don't miss client project requests from Fiverr.

- Ask your clients to reward your work with five-star reviews.

- Only take on jobs you feel qualified to work on. Turn down those that don't fit your schedule.

- Don't take it personally when clients ask for revisions. It's part of the graphic design process and no reflection on your skills.

- Strive to deliver high-quality work. Don't disappoint customers with shoddy work.

- Provide quick turn-around to keep your clients happy.

Selling Drawings & Doodles

If you like to draw, this might be for you. There's a whole new world of people out there looking for unique drawings, cartoons, doodles and artwork they can use on their company logos, book covers, websites, t-shirts, coffee mugs, and more.

Even simple line drawings, goofy little cartoons, and black and white sketches can appeal to a growing pool of potential online buyers. These include website content creators, book authors, marketing managers, t-shirt and clothing sellers, sign printers, custom decal creators and others.

Most of these potential art buyers will look to sites like www.shutterstock.com, www.istock.com, www.canstock.com and http://www.fotolia.com, where they can search or browse through thousands of illustrations they can license for a fee.

Others will visit http://www.fiverr.com and search for 'drawing', 'illustration', 'cartoon', 'sketch', 'line drawing', and pay to have a custom image created for them for a fee.

Most of the drawings and illustrations on these sites are created by amateur and professional artists who wish to earn income from their work. Some are even created by children.

The image below is a good example of the kind of artwork people are buying. It's one I contracted an artist on Fiverr to create for me to use in a book I was writing.

It's a simple image that probably took the artist just a few minutes to create. But I was happy to pay to have it created, and even paid extra to get the exclusive copyright and commercial use rights.

If you can create images like the one above or like the one on the cover of this book, you could do well selling your work on the web.

Income Potential

Most sites that offer to license your images will pay you 15% to 45% of the licensing fee each time your image is licensed. Some will pay a flat rate, ranging from a few pennies to over twenty dollars per image.

Since each image can be licensed many times over, it's possible to earn repeat income from each of your images. However, unless you upload a large number of images and unless they are licensed often, your earnings will be minimal. Still, having the right images on these sites could be a positive revenue source.

Another option is to join http://www.fiverr.com and offer to create custom drawings and illustrations. This allows you to showcase your work to potential clients and reach customers who are specifically looking for the kinds of illustrations you can create.

You are able to choose clients to work with, the prices you charge, the format your illustrations will be delivered in, and the timetable in which the work will be created.

Having your images on licensing sites as well as offering custom images on Fiverr increases your potential income without increasing your start-up costs or workload.

In most cases, the revenue from image licensing and custom illustrations will not be enough to rely on as your sole source of income – unless you become well known and sought after.

Tools Needed

To license illustrations and drawings, you'll need:

- The exclusive ownership rights to the images you want to license. If you didn't create it yourself, you probably don't own the rights and can't sell or license it to others.

- Illustrations that can be provided in .jpg or .png file formats. This means you'll need a computer and an internet connection.

- If you draw images on paper, you'll need a way to convert the images to a digital format, You can do this with a flatbed scanner connected to your computer.

- If you prefer to work digitally, you may want a Wacom type drawing pad or a tablet computer where you can draw directly on the screen.

- You may also want an image editing program like Photoshop, or Photoshop Elements to adjust your illustrations before uploading them.

- You may also want free programs like FotoSketcher (http://fotosketcher.com/) that can help turn your photos into illustrations and art.

Getting Started

To get started, you'll want to visit the various photo and illustration licensing sites and sign up as a contributor. Most of these sites will allow you to sign up without having to provide examples of your work, but some sites do require you to upload at least one image.

The sites you'll probably want to sign up with include:

- https://www.dreamstime.com/sell-stock-photos-images
- https://submit.shutterstock.com/
- http://www.istockphoto.com/
- http://www.fotolia.com/
- http://www.crestock.com/
- https://www.foap.com/
- https://www.stockimo.com/
- http://www.fiverr.com

In addition to the above sites, you might want to sell your images on coffee mugs and t-shirts. Sites that make it easy to do that include:

- http://www.cafepress.com
- http://www.sunfrog.com
- http://www.teespring.com
- https://merch.amazon.com/landing

Pros

If you like drawing and have a computer and internet connection, licensing your images on the stock image sites is an easy and trouble free way to generate income.

It's a 'set it and forget it' kind of business. You upload your drawings or illustrations, and your part is done. No checking back each day, no need to stay connected to the internet, no schedules to worry about.

If you offer custom illustrations via Fiverr, you will earn more per job but will have to check your email more often (at least twice a day) and work to meet the client's schedule. But if you stick with the kinds of illustrations that you can turn out quickly, it shouldn't be a problem.

If you apply your illustrations to tee shirts at TeeSpring, CafePress, and SunFrog, it'll take you about thirty minutes to set up an account, and after that, all the work is done for you. Income from tee shirt sales can grow if the shirt goes viral.

The shirt sites do all the work including printing, taking orders, and shipping to customers. You get paid at the end of each month.

Cons

Unless you upload a lot of illustrations and those illustrations are licensed often, you won't make a lot of money – unless you find corporate clients willing to pay more for exclusive images or you specialize in illustrating books.

There are a lot of competing illustrations and images, including many that are free, and unless yours are priced higher and are liked by customers, they may not earn any income.

Tips for Success

- Position yourself to appeal to the kind of customers who will pay more. For example, those looking for illustrations for children's books. You'll sell multiple images per client and earn more per image as you can charge more for the commercial use license.

- Offer to create illustrations for company logos. These custom illustrations will earn more. Do this on http://www.fiverr.com.

- Offer to create poster art. Again, do this via your http://www.fiverr.com account.

- Review the illustration ads on http://www.fiverr.com and create similar ads for illustration work that is within your skill set.

- When uploading images to stock image sites, include keywords which describe the elements of the image, making it easier to find when customers search.

- Review the top selling images on sites like www.Shutterstock.com to learn what sells best.

Proofreader / Editor Gigs

If you have good English skills and feel comfortable proofreading and editing documents written by others, you could be earning money as a proofreader and/or editor.

This might be an ideal way to generate income while on the road, as all you need is an internet connection, a computer, and good language skills.

Typically, you can expect to earn twenty dollars for every 5,000 words you edit. This fee varies, depending on the type of document and the type of editing. For example, resumes, sales letters and ad copy, usually call for a higher price since more work is involved.

Potential customers with editing work, will contact you via a free ad you can post offering editing services at http://www.fiverr.com. Those who contact you will tell you about the document they need proofread and edited. You decide whether you want to take on the project and if so, what you'll charge and how long it'll take you to do it.

If the client agrees to your terms, they pay up front via Fiverr escrow, and when the project is complete and delivered, Fiverr releases the payment to you.

While $20 per 5,000 words doesn't sound like a lot of money, taking on longer documents like short stories and books can pay a lot more. For example, one of the editors I used to proof and edit a novel charged me six hundred dollars.

Do two of those a month, and you earn over a thousand dollars.

Getting Started

To get started as a proofreader or editor, you'll need a PayPal account (so you can get paid), an account at http://www.fiverr.com (so you can find clients), and an MS Word compatible word processing program so you can edit the documents your clients provide.

You may also want proofreading and editing software like Grammarly or Ginger.

You'll also need to be proficient in the language of the documents you are working on and have above average spelling and reading comprehension skills.

There are different kinds of editing, so it's important to know the difference between editing and proofreading, and decide which you're qualified to do.

Here's an overview:

- **Proofreading** is the most common form of editing. Minor errors are corrected, such as verb tense, use of units like ml or millimeter, use of numbers and words such as "5" or "five". Also included are capitalization and punctuation errors such as commas, semicolons, colons, periods, dashes, and apostrophes. And of course, spelling and word usage mistakes like to/too, laid/layed and affect/effect for example.

- **Copy editing** involves the editor correcting grammar, style, repetition, word usage, etc. Sometimes combined with proofreading as it can be hard to draw the line between the two.

- **Substantive or development editing** is the most extensive and expensive. A document, usually a book, is reviewed for problems of organization and coherence. Work may include rewriting or moving blocks of text or chapters from one section to another.

Income Potential

Most small proofreading jobs covering only spelling and punctuation for a thousand words or less won't generate much income. But often, clients will pay extra for additional editing and quick turn-around. This usually brings up the price to twenty dollars for one thousand to three thousand words.

Prices go up quickly for longer documents, business reports, resumes, short stories and novels.

If you limit yourself to a few small projects a month, you could conceivably earn five hundred dollars or more per month.

Start-up Costs

If you already have a computer with occasional internet access and an MS Word compatible word processing program, there really aren't any out-of-pocket start-up costs. You will need to sign up with http://www.fiverr.com, but there's no cost to do so.

After signing up with Fiverr, you'll want to post your jobs wanted ad (which costs you nothing). Search for 'proofreading/editor' to see the ads of others, and use those as a guide for your own.

Tools Needed

As mentioned above, you'll need a computer, MS Word or compatible word processing program (OpenOffice Writer,

LibreOffice Writer) with a strong spelling and punctuation checking feature.

You'll also need to learn to use the 'record changes' feature in your word processing program so your clients can see what you have changed.

If working on longer documents, you may want to invest in a professional proof-reading and editing program like Grammarly or Ginger. These can help you quickly find spelling, punctuation and grammar errors.

Pros

If you have strong language skills, editing work might come easily to you. You can do it from anywhere in the world, choose the projects you want to accept, set your own prices and schedule.

Cons

Unless you are able to secure longer documents to edit, your income will be limited by the small amount you'll earn for lower word count material. If your language skills are weak, your clients may not accept your work, and you may not get paid.

Tips for Success

- **Offer premium editing and proofreading services** and set the prices you charge to reflect the higher quality work and fast turn-around you can provide.

- **Create a confidence inspiring ad** that shows your credentials and why customers should trust you with their work.

- **Avoid misspellings and typos in your ad** at Fiverr. (I found several in aspiring proofreader ads.)

- **Check your email every few hours to make sure you don't miss client project requests** from Fiverr.

- **Ask your clients to reward your work with five-star reviews.** This will lead to more customers in the future.

- **Offer more than just proofreading and editing services.** For those who aren't professional writers, choose phrases like the following to describe your services: Correct Spelling, Grammar, Punctuation, Awkward Phrasing, Readability, Tense Continuity, Continuity of Thought

- **Don't rely on just income from your proofreading and editing services.** Have other projects going on as well, like writing your own book.

Licensing your Photos

If you have a smart phone or camera and are traveling around the country in your RV or camper, chances are good you'll have many opportunities to capture exceptional photos. Instead of just letting those photos go to waste, you could be generating income from them.

There are hundreds of thousands of websites, publishers, writers, printers and news services looking for photos to license and use. Most will look to sites like www.shutterstock.com, www.istock.com, www.canstock.com and http://www.fotolia.com, where they can search or browse through thousands of photos which they can license for use in their work.

The photos on these sites are uploaded by amateur and professional photographers who wish to earn income from their images.

It's easy to get started selling your photos on these sites. There's usually no start-up costs, you can upload your photos to several different sites, and you always retain full copyright ownership of your photos.

Income Potential

Most sites that offer to license your photos will pay you 15% to 45% of the licensing fee each time your photo is licensed. Some will pay a flat rate, ranging from a few pennies to over twenty dollars per photo.

Since each photo can be licensed many times over, it is possible to earn repeat income from each of your images.

However, unless you have a lot of photos and unless they are licensed often, your earnings will be minimal. Still, having the right photos on these sites can be a positive revenue source.

In most cases, the revenue from photo licensing will not be enough to rely on as your sole source of income. However, if you capture a spectacular image or one that publications want to use, it can pay extremely well.

Tools Needed

To license photos, you'll need a camera or smart phone that can shoot 12 megapixel or greater images. You may also want a photo editing program like Photoshop, Photoshop Elements or LightRoom to crop and edit photos.

You'll also need an internet connection so you can upload the photos to the various photo licensing services you choose to work with.

Getting Started

To get started, visit the various photo licensing sites and sign up as a contributor. Most will allow you to sign up without having to provide examples of your work, but some sites require you to upload at least one photo demonstrating your photo skills.

The sites you'll probably want to sign up with include:

- http://submit.shutterstock.com/

- http://www.istockphoto.com/

- http://www.fotolia.com/

- http://www.canstockphoto.com/ (must submit images)

- http://www.crestock.com/

- https://www.foap.com/ (works with smart phone)

- https://www.stockimo.com/ (smart phone app)

- https://www.twenty20.com/

- http://www.alamy.com/

- https://www.eyeem.com/

Several of the above sites offer phone apps that make it easy to upload photos from your phone as soon as you shoot them. Most sites prefer you upload from your computer though.

Pros

If you have a decent phone or camera that can shoot 12 megapixel or better photos and you understand the basic principles of good photography and you shoot lots of photos, selling on re-licensing websites makes sense.

You'll have a good excuse to shoot more photos and maybe even a better excuse to get a higher quality camera or lens (or phone).

Cons

Unless you upload a lot of quality photos or shoot the kind of images customers want to license, you won't make a lot of money. Even if your photos are licensed, they'll usually pay less than twenty dollars per use.

To make a decent income, you'll need a lot of photos that get licensed often.

There are a lot of competing photos, and unless yours really stand out or depict scenes that aren't readily available elsewhere, they may not earn any income.

Tips for Success

- Shoot the kind of photos that are most likely to be licensed. Landscapes, landmarks, weather, seasonal, travel, nature, animals, holidays, sunsets, sunrises, moon phases, sky, clouds, evocative and historical.

- Never include people or trademarked images in your photos. These pose privacy and trademark problems and won't be accepted at most photo licensing sites – unless they are of public figures.

- If you get the opportunity to shoot candid photos of public figures (e.g. actors or politicians), you may want to do so. Photos of actors doing things they shouldn't can pay extremely well.

- Shoot photos that can be used in calendars, ads, book covers, magazine articles, websites, posters, brochures, etc.

- Shoot high-resolution jpeg images (most sites require a minimum 12-megabyte uncompressed jpeg).

- Upload the same photo to several photo-sharing sites – unless you sell the exclusive use rights.

- When uploading images, include keywords that describe the

elements of the image, making it easier to find it when customers search.

- Review the top selling photos on sites like Shutterstock.com to see what kind of photos sell best. Then try to shoot those kinds of photos.

- Review the Shutterstock blog to find recent photo trends and tips on how to get better photos. Find it at https://www.shutterstock.com/blog/category/tips-and-tutorials

- Download the free ShutterStock Guide to Success https://submit.shutterstock.com/guides/success

- Download and install the photo selling smart phone apps listed at http://www.makeuseof.com/tag/make-money-smartphone-photography/

- If you capture a news event, upload the original unaltered image to Alamy within 24 hours of the event. They will license it to the news media for you. Details at http://www.alamy.com/contributor/how-to-sell-news-images/best-place-to-sell-live-news-images/

- Try to carry a camera with you everywhere you go as you never know when a great photo opportunity might present itself.

Tee Shirt Designer/Promoter

This is one of the easiest businesses to start. It takes a few minutes to get going, there's no startup cost, no web site required, no selling, no inventory to maintain, and you can run it from anywhere in the world. It's a perfect business when living on the road.

Here's how it works.

I was surfing the Florida RV Camping group on Facebook and saw a posting that included an image of an RV related t-shirt. The shirt had a funny saying on the front, and the posting had a link to where you could order the shirt in your size.

Under the post, I saw that a lot of people had clicked the 'like' button and there were a few messages from people saying they'd just ordered one of the shirts.

I saw the same shirt posted in many of the other Facebook RV groups I follow. Most of these groups have three to ten thousand followers – and a lot of them would see the post about the t-shirt.

It's likely a small percentage of those who saw the t-shirt ordered one. But if only 1% ordered, it could mean 500 orders – in a single day. That's a lot of sales and income for the person who created the shirt.

I wondered how much trouble it would be to duplicate what the poster had done. I wanted to know how he got the shirt created, who was printing it, who took the orders, and how much it cost to ship.

I did a little digging, and it didn't take long to learn that getting into this kind of business was drop dead easy. There was zero cost to get started, and all the heavy lifting was done by one company.

Tee Shirt Design Business

Companies like Tee-Spring and SunFrog will let you upload your t-shirt design, print the shirt for you, create a sales page, accept customer orders, process credit card payments, and ship shirts to paying customers. Each month, they'll send you profit from shirt sales.

Both of these companies have free online tools to make it easy to create t-shirt designs and build marketing campaigns to promote the shirts — all at no cost to you, the shirt designer.

Coming up with the t-shirt design doesn't have to be difficult. Just find a hobby niche and create a design for people in that niche, then post a link to the shirt's sales page on TeeSpring or SunFrog in Facebook and Pinterest groups the people in that niche follow.

When they follow the link to the shirt's sales page and place an order, you earn a profit.

Income Potential

The people who do well in the shirt design business using TeeSpring or SunFrog can earn several thousand dollars a month. Most won't earn that much, but some will.

If you design and promote several shirts, your chances of earning decent money increase.

There are no out-of-pocket costs to getting into this business and no chance of losing money. Your biggest investment is the time you spend designing and promoting your shirts.

Getting Started

To get started in the tee-shirt business, you'll want to create a free creators account at:

- https://teespring.com/

- https://www.sunfrog.com/

After you sign up, you'll want to read and agree to their terms of service and then either upload your design or use their free online design tool to create one on their site.

After you set a price for the shirt, a sales page will be created for you, and you can then post links to that page on social media groups.

Tools needed

When it comes to shirt designs, you can either use graphic tools already on your computer or use the tools that the design sites provide.

I prefer to use Photoshop Elements to create designs, but that's just my personal preference.

The advantage of using the tools provided on shirt design sites is that you can see what the design will look like on a shirt, like the example below.

Pros

Because it costs nothing to start your t-shirt design business at the two sites mentioned above, you have very little to lose when getting into this business.

If you can come up with a design that people want to buy and wear, you can do well.

Cons

If you aren't computer literate, don't have internet access or don't have a PayPal account (to receive your monthly earnings), being in the t-shirt design business probably isn't for you.

While it is easy to design shirts using the sites mentioned above, it will be up to you to market the shirts by posting links on Facebook, Pinterest, and other social media groups.

If you are not social media savvy, this will make it difficult for you to market the shirts.

Tips for Success

- To get ideas for shirt designs that sell, check out the list (with pictures) of the one hundred best selling t-shirts of all times at https://goo.gl/srKBRC.

- Watch the design and marketing videos provided free by SunFrog at http://academy.sunfrog.com/.

- Get acquainted with and use the free design tools provided by SunFrog and TeeSpring.

- Expand your offerings from t-shirts to include hoodies, coffee mugs, and more with SunFrog.com.

- Join and regularly visit Facebook and other social media groups related to hobbies you are interested in. Keep up with the posts and when you see a trend, create a t-shirt for it and post a link to the shirt in related social media groups.

- Don't abuse your posting privileges by posting sales pages too frequently in any one Facebook group.

- When you hear a phrase that you think would look good on a t-shirt, write it down, so you remember to use it.

- Never use a trademark word or phrase in your t-shirt designs.

- Shirts with humorous phrases sell better than political slogans.

- Shirts that refer to places can sell well. Best-selling t-shirt of all time – I love New York.

- Don't be discouraged if your first few design efforts don't make the profits you expect. The more you work at it, the better your chance of success.

Freelance Gigs

If you check the 'Gigs' category of Craigslist for almost any area it serves, you'll find lots of temporary jobs. These can include painting, day labor, yard work, moving boxes, house cleaning, trash removal, tree trimming, TV show extras, models, and just about anything else you can imagine.

Income Potential

Since most of these jobs are temporary, you usually won't earn much. But almost all will pay at least ten dollars an hour, and most will pay in cash.

Some of these jobs can lead to other higher paying opportunities from the same employer after they find out whether you are a reliable worker or not.

You won't get rich doing day labor jobs, but it can be a good way to quickly raise cash to help cover your living expenses. Plus you meet people who might know about other available jobs.

Tools Needed

Most of these day labor jobs only require a strong back and a willingness to work. Some will require you to wear work clothes, have heavy gloves and boots. Others only need you to show up in tennis shoes, shorts and a t-shirt. Find out before you go.

Getting Started

To find these kinds of jobs, go to www.craigslist.org on your computer, click the city and state you are in, and then look in the 'gigs' category.

Find jobs that look interesting or fit your skills and reply to the posting. A phone call usually is the best way to make contact.

Also check https://www.peopleperhour.com for freelance jobs near you.

Pros

• Jobs usually pay in cash

• No long-term commitment

• Employment is often immediate

• Can lead to more opportunities

Cons

• Can involve heavy lifting

• Can require you to work in hot or cold weather

• Not always available in all locations

Mining Semi-Precious Stones

I call it 'treasure camping.'

It's when you camp at or near a 'dig your own' gem or crystal mine. You pay a small fee to go in and dig all day, and you get to keep what you find.

In many cases, if you know what you're doing, you can end up with hundreds and sometimes thousands of dollars worth of gems and semi-precious stones that you get to take away with you at no additional cost.

These finds, when cleaned up, can often be sold to New Age shops, jewelry makers, and on eBay or Etsy.

You'll find 'dig your own' mines spread across the country, from east coast to west. By following the seasons, you can usually visit a mine when the digging weather is best.

For example, in the spring and fall, you might want to visit the crystal mines found in the Ouachita Mountains in Arkansas. These are concentrated in a fifty-mile band from Hot Springs to Mt Ida.

A good place to start is the Ron Coleman Crystal Mine in Jessieville, Arkansas. For twenty dollars a day, you gain access to their open pit mine and can keep all the crystals you find. Even better, they offer a modern RV park for campers, with a daily rate of $12.50, which includes electric and water hookups. The monthly rate is $300, and the park is just a few steps from the mine. (Find details at http://colemanquartz.com/).

There are several other crystal mines within a few miles, a nearby Walmart Superstore, restaurants, and fast food places. The area is just a thirty-minute drive to world famous Hot Springs National Park.

When you get your fill of quartz crystal mining, you can head over to the Crater of Diamonds State Park in Murfreesboro, Arkansas, where for $10 a day you can look for diamonds and keep all you find.

And yes, people do find diamonds there. The largest so far is over 80 carats, but the average size is about half a carat. These diamonds range in color from white, clear, yellow, brown and black, and are worth anywhere from a few hundred dollars to millions.

Crater of Diamonds State Park has 47 full hookup sites as well as tent sites. Camping prices start at $12.00 a night for tents. Find out more at http://www.craterofdiamondsstatepark.com

These are just two of the many places in the US where you can 'treasure camp.' In some mines, you can dig for emeralds, rubies, and sapphires. In others, you can pan for gold. In almost all the mines, you pay an entrance fee, get to dig all day and keep what you find.

I've camped and mined at several these places, and you can read about some of them in my articles at:

- http://www.bmyers.com/public/Crystal_mining.cfm
- http://www.bmyers.com/public/Crater_of_Diamonds.cfm

Income Potential

When digging for gems and semi-precious stones, it helps to know what to look for and what your potential buyers are looking for in terms of quality, color, and size.

For example, with quartz crystals, clear jewelry points are much more valuable than larger milky pieces. Double terminated points and clear crystals with inclusions (especially water) are highly sought after. Broken pieces have little more than yard-art value and are not usually worth lugging up out of the mines.

With rubies, emeralds, and sapphires, stone color and quality are as important as size. Almost all will have value, some quite a bit more than others. Speak to the mine operators and ask what you should be looking for.

Same goes with diamonds. At the Crater of Diamonds State Park, Rangers are happy to show you what to look for and provide examples of actual diamonds found in the mine. You'll know when someone finds a diamond there, as the Rangers ring a bell to let everyone know one was found. (Several were found the two days I was there.)

No matter which mine you visit, chances are good you'll come away with at least a hundred dollars in valuable stones. In some cases, the value will be much higher.

When these finds are resold as either raw stones on in the form of jewelry (covered later in this book), profits can be substantial.

Start-up Costs

The big costs when it comes to treasure camping are the fuel costs to get to the mines, the daily entrance fees, and nightly camping fees.

Most mines charge a $10 to $20 daily 'dig your own' fee, but some, especially the emerald, ruby and sapphire mines, charge more.

For example, the Emerald Hollow Mine in North Carolina has a $25 daily fee for sluicing, creeking and digging. They also offer pre-dug buckets you can go through. Prices depend on the size and quality of bucket contents. Find out more at http://www.emeraldhollowmine.com

Tools Needed

Most mines are open fields which have been plowed or opened with excavators. To find gems, you'll need a digging tool (a long handle screwdriver is ideal), heavy gloves, waterproof boots, and a bag or basket to carry your finds in.

If you don't bring your own digging tools, most mines have tools for rent.

Pros

The adventure of being outdoors on a quest to find treasure is reason enough for some people to visit 'dig your own' mines. If you go in good weather (not too hot and not too cold), it can be a fun and educational experience.

If you stick with it or tag along with experienced miners, chances are good you'll come away with some valuable gems or semi-precious stones you can sell for a profit.

Cons

When mining for gems, you'll be working outdoors, often bent over or digging in the dirt. If you misjudge the weather, you'll be hot and miserable or cold and wet. The quality of the finds can vary daily, as the operators open new areas and bring up tailings for miners to sift through.

If you don't enjoy spending time outdoors while digging in the dirt, this won't be for you. Most mines offer to refund your mining fee if you don't find anything, but there is no guarantee you'll find ten times the cost of the entry fee.

Tips for Success

- Plan on getting dirty! Bring a change of clothes and shoes, an old towel or two, and sunscreen and bug spray.

- Wear work boots with a deep tread as dig sites can get slick at times.

- Wear heavy gloves. Crystals and gem shards are sharp and can cut unprotected fingers.

- Wear polarized sunglasses. They help pick out shiny stones in the dirt.

- Wear knee pads. These will save your knees as you dig.

- Bring your own tools. This will save you a tool rental fee at the mine. Usually, a long-handled screwdriver and a plastic bucket are all you need. In some mines, a rock hammer is useful.

- Carry old newspapers in your bucket. Wrap your finds with paper to prevent them from being chipped as you move around the mine.

- Look for the easy finds on top of the ground – this is where most of the diamonds are discovered.

- Look for and follow the gem rich veins in crystal and gem mines. The veins are where you find the good stuff.

- Before going to a mine, ask locals which mines are currently producing the best stones. Some mines are not worth visiting, many are tourist attractions without a real mine. Avoid them.

- Before driving to a mine in an RV or camper, check the road conditions. Some mines are located many miles down unimproved dirt roads, not suitable for travel in aa RV or camper.

- While at mines, ask the staff what is the best way to clean the gems and stones you find. The info they offer on cleaning can save you a lot of time and trouble.

- Visit New Age shops to see what stones they sell and what prices they are asking. Use this as a guide for the kind and size of stones you look for.

- Visit the websites of mines and find the dates and hours the mines are open. Many are seasonal and close for the winter.

- Visit the Facebook pages of the mines you plan to visit to see what kinds of things are being found. Example: https://www.facebook.com/twincreekmine/

- Check out the listings and photos of gemstones that can be found in each state at http://geology.com/gemstones/states/

- Read http://www.goldandgemgazette.com/gem-hunting-my-side-job-as-a-gold-miner/

Places to find Gems and semi-precious stones

Here is a partial list of mines you can visit. In areas where a mine is listed, there are usually other mines nearby. Check with locals to find out which are the best.

- Herkimer Diamond Mines, Middleville, NY http://herkimerdiamond.com/

- Alabama Gold Camp http://alabamagoldcamp.com/

- Cherokee Ruby & Sapphire Mine, Franklin, NC http://cherokeerubymine.com/

- Gem Mountain, Spruce Pine, NC
  http://www.gemmountain.com/

- Emerald Hollow Mine, Hiddenite, NC
  http://www.hiddenitegems.com

- Diamond Hill Mine, Abbeville, SC
  http://diamondhillmine.com/informationcost/

- Gold n Gem Grubbin, Cleveland, GA
  http://www.goldngemgrubbinstore.com/index.html

- Graves Mountain (Lincolnton, GA)
  http://www.gamineral.org/ft/commercial/ftgravesmain.html

- Crater of Diamonds State Park, Murfreesboro, AR
  http://www.craterofdiamondsstatepark.com

- Ron Coleman Crystal Mine, Jessieville, Ark
  http://colemanquartz.com/

- Twin Creek Crystal Mine, Mt Ida, AR
  https://www.facebook.com/twincreekmine/

- Wegner Crystal Mine, Mt Ida, AR
  http://www.wegnercrystalmines.com

- Board Campground Crystal Mine, Mena, AR
  http://www.boardcampcampground.com

- Woodward Ranch Agate Mine, Alpine, TX
  http://woodwardranch.com/

- Morefield Gem Mine, Amelia, VA

http://morefieldgemmine.com/

- Spencer Opal Mines, Spencer ID
  https://spenceropalmines.com/you-can-dig-it/

- Gem Mountain, Philipsburg, MT
  http://www.gemmountainmt.com/

- Spectrum Sunstone Mine, Plush, OR
  http://www.highdesertgemsandminerals.com

- Himalaya Tourmaline Mine, Santa Ysabel, CA
  http://www.highdesertgemsandminerals.com/html/himalaya_mi
  ne_dig.html

- Jade Cove Trail, Big Sur, CA
  http://www.hikinginbigsur.com/hikes_jadecove.html

- California State Gem Mine, Coalinga, CA
  http://calstategemmine.com/

- Rainbow Ridge Opal Mine, Virgin Valley, NV
  http://nevadaopal.com/

- Rock Hound State Park, Deming, NM
  http://www.emnrd.state.nm.us/spd/rockhoundstatepark.html

Research Resources

- List of fee mines in the US - http://rocktumbler.com/blog/fee-
  mining-and-digging-sites/

- http://www.geologyin.com/

- Top Spots for Gem Hunting
  http://www.geologyin.com/2017/02/part-ii-top-spots-for-gem-hunting-in-us.html#iJGXlc4iDcS6soQx.99

- Photos of many of the mines listed above
  https://www.gemsociety.org/article/mined-in-america/

Digging Fossils

In the previous chapter, I called it 'Treasure Camping.'

It's when you camp near a 'dig your own' mine. You pay a small fee to gain access to the mining area, and you get to keep what you find there.

That earlier chapter was about digging crystals, gems and semi-precious stones. In this chapter, we'll cover another kind of precious stone: fossils.

Fossils are the remains or impressions of prehistoric organisms preserved in rock. Most are many millions of years old and are found in sizes ranging from smaller than a penny to larger than a delivery truck.

Depending on the size, rarity and quality, fossils can have a market value of just a few dollars to hundreds of thousands or even millions.

Fossils can be sold to collectors, mineral and gem wholesalers and retailers, schools, museums and jewelry makers.

At the 'dig your own fossil' mines, you pay a few dollars and have a pretty good chance of finding fossils that far exceed your admission price. Most mines allow you to keep everything you find – unless otherwise noted.

What you do with your finds is up to you. Often individual pieces can be sold for a significant profit.

The fossils you find at these places will typically be ancient trilobites, dinosaur bones and teeth, prehistoric dung, sea creatures, plants and birds. Most will be embedded in shale or some other kind of rock.

Digging fossils at the mines usually involves using a stone hammer and breaking rock slabs looking for prime specimens.

In many cases, if you stick with it long enough and know what you're doing, you can end up with several thousand dollars worth of fossils that you can take away from the mine at no cost (other than the initial admission fee).

Profit Potential

Fossil prices are all over the board. Smaller, common trilobite fossils can bring twenty dollars. Larger specimens can sometimes sell for several hundred dollars.

An intact dinosaur fossil, even a small one, can sell for hundreds or thousands of dollars.

A good day at the mine can have you leaving with finds worth thousands. Or it can be just a sweaty day pounding slate and not finding anything worthwhile.

Start-up Costs

The big expenses involved in digging fossils include:

- The **cost of traveling to the mine** – while fossil dig sites are found in several states, some of the best are in remote areas and require a bit of travel. Figure fuel and camping expenses in your costs.

- **Admission fees** – Fees charged by commercial fossil dig sites can range from $30 to $100 per day. Mines with the best fossils usually charge more.

Tools Needed

Digging fossils is usually a matter of breaking rocks using a chisel edge rock hammer. These can be purchased at hardware stores, online or at the dig site. Figure thirty dollars for one of the best – an Estwing Supreme 24 oz. Chisel Edge Rock Hammer (available on Amazon and many hardware stores).

You'll also want leather gloves, durable clothes, work boots, a sun hat, and sunscreen.

Pros

A day's dig at the right fossil site can result in the discovery of fossils that can be resold for thousands of dollars. Some of the most interesting fossil dig sites are free.

Cons

There is no guarantee that digging at any fossil site will result in valuable finds. Some state regulations at fee sites require you to hand over rare or valuable finds.

Digging involves physical labor outdoors in the sun, mostly in rocky areas.

You can spend hours bent over, pounding rocks searching for unbroken fossil specimens.

In some of the fee mines, it can cost a hundred dollars a day or more to gain access to the dig area.

Tips for Success

- To get a taste of what fossil hunting is like, visit one or more of the free dig sites (see list at the end of this chapter).

- Before visiting a 'dig for a fee' fossil operation, check their website to find the days and months of operation and the kinds of fossils being found. Check restrictions on finds (some limit you to 10 or fewer finds per day.)

- Try to schedule your fossil hunts during optimal weather. Not too hot, not too cold. The better the weather, the more you'll enjoy the dig, and the longer you'll keep at it.

- Wear suitable clothing. Long sleeve shirts, heavy pants, work boots, leather gloves and sun hat. Wear sunscreen.

- Bring refreshments, including plenty of water.

- Bring a bucket or bag to store your fossil finds. Wrap finds in newspaper to prevent chipping or breaking.

- Before visiting fossil dig sites, search sites that sell fossils to see which kinds bring the most money and are the easiest to sell. Know before you start digging what you are looking for.

- Check road conditions leading to the fossil dig sites. Some will not be suitable for travel in an RV or camper.

Resources

- Photos and descriptions of many fossil dig sites across the country
  http://nautiloid.net/fossils/sites/sites.html

- Maps and photos of free fossil dig sites
  http://www.fossilguy.com/sites/

- Public parks where you can legally hunt and remove fossils
  https://www.thoughtco.com/fossil-parks-for-hands-on-digging-1440567

Partial list of free and fee fossil dig sites.

- Warfield Fossil Quarries, Thayne, WY
  http://www.fossilsafari.com/

- U-DIG Fossils (trilobites), Delta, UT
  http://www.u-digfossils.com/

- Florissant Fossil Quarry, Florissant, CO
  http://florissantfossils.tripod.com/

- Ulrich's Fossil Gallery, Kemmerer, WY
  http://ulrichsfossilgallery.com/

- Blue Moon Quarry, Kemmerer, WY
  http://promiselandfossils.com/BlueMoon.html

- Zeder Co International, Kemmerer, WY
  http://www.zederco.com/digging-fossils.html

- Fossil Lake, Kemmerer, WY
  http://piscesprehistoric.com/pay_dig_agreement.html

- Fossil Expeditions, Peace River, FL
  http://www.fossilexpeditions.com/
- Big Brook Fossil Site (free), NJ
  http://www.njfossils.net/
- Montour Fossil Pit (free), Danville, PA
  https://montourpreserve.org/fossil-pit/

Metal Detecting

When writing about treasure camping, I'd be remiss if I didn't include a chapter on metal detecting. The reason I say this is not only have I spent hundreds of hours metal detecting for treasure, I've produced a number of videos showing what I do and how much I've found. I've even created a DVD on the subject, 'Metal Detecting Florida Beaches', which is available on Amazon.

You may be wondering; how can you make any money metal detecting?

The best answer is, you have to detect in areas where treasures (rings, jewelry, gold and coins) and other goodies can be found.

In the years I've been metal detecting, I've found hundreds of rings (some with diamonds), bracelets, gold and silver chains, a few watches, thousands of coins, cameras, car keys, knives and just about every other kind of metal object you can imagine.

I mostly detect beaches and swimming holes, where people get into the water and lose rings and such. I also detect old home sites, campgrounds (where legal), city parks, and public recreational areas.

While you won't get rich with a metal detector, you are likely to find some interesting things, including some that might be quite valuable. Here's one of the things I found.

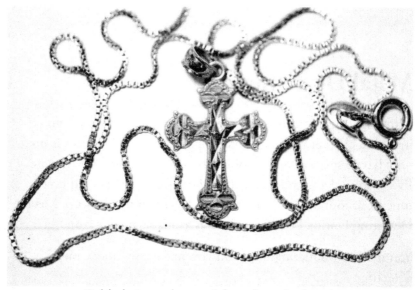

Gold chain and cross I found on the beach

Profit Potential

Metal detecting should be looked at as a hobby, not as a way to make money. In most cases, you'll spend many hours searching before you find anything of value. You could go fifty hours or more finding only pull tabs and bottle caps.

Or you could get lucky and find a Spanish Reale – a silver or gold coin from one of the eleven ships of the Spanish Treasure Fleet of 1715 which sank off Florida's east coast. Coins and jewelry from that wreck are still being found on the beaches to this day.

Most likely though, you'll find more modern objects. Lots of coins and pocket change, costume jewelry worn by beach-goers, class rings, gold and silver chains, and objects forgotten or left behind by visitors to the area you are detecting in.

Coins found with metal detector

Unless you are extremely lucky or come upon high yield 'virgin territory' unsearched by others, you won't get rich doing this. However, you will get plenty of exercise, a nice tan, and an excuse to walk on the beach with your detector.

Tools Needed

To get started metal detecting, you'll need a quality metal detector and a digging tool. If detecting the beaches, you'll also want a long-handled sand scoop. You'll want appropriate outdoor wear, a hat, and sunscreen.

You will want a pair of headphones for your detector so when it sounds a tone letting you know you've discovered something, you don't disturb or alert others nearby.

Me on the beach with a metal detector

A good beginning detector would be the Garrett Ace 250. You can find these new for around $215. Used ones can sometimes be found on Craigslist or eBay for around $150.

If you purchase a new detector from Amazon or www.kellyco.com, you'll almost always get a package deal that includes the detector, a case, a coil cover, a digging tool, and headphones.

Start-up Costs

Figure around $250 to get started in metal detecting with a decent detector like the Garrett Ace 250. If you want to spend more, get a Garrett AT Pro (waterproof) for around $600.

I've had several detectors, some costing more than a thousand dollars, and my two favorites are the Ace 250 ($220) and the AT Pro ($600).

Pros

As mentioned above, metal detecting should be seen as a hobby where you can get exercise, a tan, and have a chance of ending the day with a valuable or semi-valuable treasure – or a pocket full of pull tabs.

If you visit areas where there's a lot of recreational activity, beaches, swimming holes, ski slopes (in the summer), outdoor concerts, etc., metal detecting can produce some interesting results.

Cons

You'll have to spend at least two hundred dollars to get a decent metal detector and tools.

There's no guarantee you'll find anything of value when you detect.

You'll usually have to put in a lot of practice hours before you learn to use your detector and start finding things of value.

It can be a big waste of time if you don't enjoy being outdoors searching for treasure.

Tips for Success

- Start with a decent detector. The cheap ones found in big box stores are a waste of money. They miss valuable items that a better detector will find.

- Always use headphones when detecting. These help in pinpointing targets and won't annoy or attract attention from other people that might be nearby.

- Always get permission before detecting if there is any doubt that it is legal to do so. Never detect on private property without getting permission.

- Carry two finds bags. One for valuable items and one for trash. Carry away the trash.

- If you dig holes to uncover objects, always cover the holes before you leave.

- Be wary of showing your finds to strangers who may approach and ask to see what you've found. Most are just curious, but some may see a chance to grab and run off with what you've found.

- If you find an obviously valuable or personal object, try to find the owner. Returning valuables to their rightful owner is the right thing to do.

- Clean your detector after every use. Don't leave it in your car on a hot day. Always carry an extra set of fresh batteries.

- Dig all tones. You won't know whether the detector has found another pull tab or a valuable platinum ring unless you dig it.

- Watch videos on YouTube to learn how to use your detector in different settings.

- Visit the forums at http://www.treasurenet.com/ to find tips and tricks from other detectors.

- If you find valuable items to sell, take them to a coin shop or gold buyer. Avoid pawn shops as they usually pay the least.

Making and Selling Jewelry

If you treasure camp as mentioned in the previous chapters and come away with semi-precious stones, fossils, and interesting coins, you'll have the main ingredients needed to make jewelry that can be sold online on eBay or Etsy, or sold to retailers or at craft shows and flea markets.

The easiest kind of jewelry to make is wire-wrapped pendants. No special tools are required other than small needle and round nose pliers. You'll also need silver or copper wire (available online or at most craft stores), your time, and a stone, fossil or coin.

Using the silver or copper wire wrap, you securely bind the featured stone or coin and add a jump ring to attach the item to a bracelet or chain.

Created wire-wrapped jewelry is relatively easy, and you can find videos on YouTube showing you how to do it.

Income Potential

Wire wrapped crystal pendants will sell for $10 and up, with no real upper limit. The price depends on the quality and uniqueness of the item, the quality of the wrap and whether a chain is included and what it's made of: silver, copper, brass, or a base metal.

Jewelry made from other semi-precious stones such as rubies and sapphires will fetch much higher prices.

Start-up Costs

The three biggest expenses in making jewelry are the:

- **Cost of the item to be wrapped** - If you acquired the objects to be wrapped by finding them as mentioned in the treasure camping chapters, your costs are minimal.

- **Cost of the wire wrap** - $6.00 for six yards of silver wire

- **The time required to wrap and mount an item** – this will depend on your skill level and experience. After your first few mounts, you should be able to create a wire wrapped pendant in twenty minutes or less.

Tools Needed

Simple wire wrapped pendants require no tools other than your fingers. However, my wife who occasionally makes wire wrapped pendants recommends having these to assist the creative process:

- Small needle nose pliers, round and flat head
- Lightweight wire cutters
- An assortment of nail files for smoothing cut edges

You can find these at most hardware, craft, home supply and big box stores for a few dollars each.

Pros

Creating wire-wrapped jewelry is a relatively easy and inexpensive way to double or triple the value of crystals and stones you find while treasure camping. The finished jewelry can be sold online or to retailers. Each piece is easy to pack and ship to customers, and each piece is unique.

You can make and sell jewelry from any location, and it can be done in your spare time and on the schedule you set.

Each piece can be a unique one of a kind creation, and it can be customized to meet the demands of the buying public.

Cons

If you don't like or aren't able to do fine work with your hands, making jewelry may not appeal to you.

If you don't have an affordable supply of crystals or semi-precious stones to mount, it might not make financial sense to buy stones from retailers and then try to sell them as jewelry.

Unless you turn out exceptional work with quality stones, you probably won't earn enough from your jewelry sales to cover all your living expenses.

Tips for Success

- Before making jewelry, check Etsy and other sites to see what kinds of gem based jewelry are selling best and in what price range. Use what you find as a guide to the kind of jewelry you might want to make and sell.

- Acquire an inventory of jewelry quality crystals and semi-precious stones you can use when making jewelry. You'll want to minimize your cost of these stones by digging them yourself (see previous chapters).

- Learn how to shoot photos of your creations so they look their best when listed online. In most cases, shooting against a black felt back helps showcase the jewelry item.

- Check with independent retailers who might be interested in purchasing jewelry from you. Especially small shops that sell to New Age customers.

- Expand your jewelry offerings by adding silver chains and bangles (which can be purchased at craft shops or on Etsy). These can add value and up the purchase price of your wares.

- Consider selling at flea markets by sharing table space with established vendors.

Picking Vintage Goods

So, my wife stopped in at a UPS store where she bumped into a guy carrying a roulette wheel. Since it isn't often that you see people walking around carrying a roulette wheel, she had to ask the guy about it.

He told her he found it at a yard sale the previous weekend. He paid twenty dollars for it after bargaining the seller down from the twenty-five-dollar asking price.

He took the roulette wheel home, shot some photos of it and put it on eBay. Four days later, it sold for two thousand dollars.

That's why he was in the UPS store carrying a roulette wheel – he needed to ship it to his buyer.

Pickers and Yard Sales

If you've watched the popular Pickers TV show, you know that the two men in the show travel around the US in their van, stopping along the way to pick (buy) used items at yard sales, collectors homes and shuttered stores.

They pay minimal prices for the items they buy, and then usually double their money when they resale them from their store or web site.

You can do the same thing. Except instead of selling from a store, you'll usually resell your 'picked' items on eBay or other online sales sites.

Visiting yard sales is a great way to get started as a picker.

Often, Grandma's and Grandpa's collectibles are being sold off by their offspring, who have no idea of their value and just want to get rid of them. The sellers see an old watch or travel alarm clock as having no value, not realizing that on eBay the items could sell for hundreds of dollars.

They might not realize that hidden in that box marked 'costume jewelry' is an 18k gold ring with a real diamond in the center. Or that string of pearls they have listed for two dollars and think is fake, are actually real and quite valuable.

And they might be happy to sell that dusty old painting of flowers for thirty dollars – not realizing it was a previously unknown Martin Johnson Heade painting worth $30 million. (True story).

While you probably won't find a million-dollar painting at a yard sale, chances are good that if you visit enough yard sales, you will find things you can buy for a few dollars and sell on eBay for a significant profit.

Of course, it helps to know what kind of items to buy, what to avoid, what sells best, and which items are the easiest to pack and ship.

To help you with that, here's a short list of items that are often found at yard sales and can usually be resold on eBay for a profit:

- **Vintage Levi's jeans,** pre-**1980** - these can often be bought for a few dollars and resold to collectors on eBay for $50 to $500 or more. The older the jeans, the better. Worn and torn jeans can often bring top dollar. (Spend a few minutes on Google to find out how to identify old Levi's before heading out on a shopping spree).

- **Vintage Levi's jean jackets** – just like vintage jeans, vintage Levi's jean jackets are prized by collectors on eBay. Finding the right one for a few dollars at a yard sale can turn into a big profit when resold on eBay.

- **1960's and older automobile license plates** – some older license plates can be quite collectible, but not all are, so you don't want to pay too much for them. Your best bet is to find these at garage and yard sales, and pay no more than a few dollars each. Be sure to buy only older plates in good condition. The older the better.

- **Vintage cowboy items** - especially spurs, chaps, holsters, lighters and leather goods. Depending on where you live, these might be hard to find. But if you ever come across spurs, chaps, and cowboy decorated items, you'll want to take a close look, and make an offer to buy. These items can bring top dollar on eBay, as long as you avoid cheap reproductions.

- **Vintage belt buckles** - who would have thought there was a strong collectible market for vintage belt buckles? But there is, and often these can go for several hundred dollars. Knowing which ones are valuable is the key. Buy the right ones at the right price, and you can do well.

- **Vintage Sports Memorabilia** – Jerseys, jackets, uniforms, and helmets from famous teams or sporting events can bring good money on eBay – but only if the items are authentic and authorized by the league.

- **Vintage Jewelry** – Look for rings, brooches, bracelets with stones held by prongs instead of glue. Study up on tips showing how to tell the difference between fake and real pearls, diamonds and gold. Try to purchase jewelry boxes full of jewelry. Get to the yard sale early to find the best deals.

- **Vintage transistor radios** - the older, art deco transistor radios from the 1930's through late 1950's can bring top dollar on eBay. Unusual color combinations, advertising pieces, leather cases, and certain brands bring the most bids.

The items above are just a few of the kinds of things that can sell well on eBay, are easy to pack and ship, and often can be bought for a few dollars at yard and garage sales.

Income Potential

While there are some amazing stories about pickers making millions of dollars from a once-in-a-lifetime find, these are few and far between. In most cases, small time pickers hope to make a profit of five times purchase price.

If they buy an item for ten dollars, they hope to be able to sell it for fifty dollars or more. This works best with smaller, inexpensive items that have collector appeal.

To make a decent profit as a picker, it helps to pick in areas where younger families are selling off their aging parents and grandparents possessions. Some areas of the country will be much better for this than others.

Retirement areas are high on the picker's preferred list, as are more affluent communities. Less ideal are areas where income has remained low for several generations.

Start-up Costs

The only real costs in becoming a picker is the time needed to visit yard and garage sales and the cash needed to buy a few items for resale.

For as little as twenty dollars and half a day picking, you could come away with a box filled with treasures that could earn hundred dollars of profit on eBay.

Tools Needed

To be a successful picker, you'll want to know what eBay buyers are looking for and what they are willing to pay. One way to do this is to search eBay's trends page, where you'll see what items are currently 'hot' or sought by buyers. You can find eBay Trends page at https://explore.ebay.com

Another useful tool when picking at yard sales is a phone app that shows what an item would sell for on eBay. There are several apps that do this, including the 'What's it Worth on eBay' app – available for Android and iPhone and currently free.

When it comes to selling the items you buy, you'll want an eBay and PayPal account, an internet connection, and a camera that can shoot decent photos.

Pros

If you like roaming yard and garage sales and are traveling in areas where higher end items are likely to found, becoming a picker for profit might be a good fit.

It helps to be able to see through the trash and find items that will appeal to collectors and buyers on eBay. It also helps to know how to bargain to get good prices from sellers.

Cons

Being a picker means going out to yard and garage sales, looking through a lot of worthless junk, and being able to select items that have high resale potential.

If you don't enjoy visiting yard sales or negotiating prices or talking to strangers or don't have the funds needed to make purchases, this probably won't be for you.

There is no guarantee of making a profit, and there is a risk that you won't be able to sell what you buy.

Tips for Success

- **Specialize** in just a few item categories. Examples could include old photos, cuff links, vintage watches, movie posters, coins, military medals, comic books, and Barbie dolls.

- **Know what an item is worth** before you buy.

- **Don't overpay** for anything. Always try to buy for pennies on the dollar.

- **Focus on smaller, easy to ship**, non-breakable items.

- **Learn to tell the difference between authentic and reproduction** items. Reproductions have minimal value

- **Resist the temptation** to buy things that you know little about.

- **Use a phone app like 'What's it worth on eBay'** to get an idea of what an item might be worth before buying.

- **Learn to take appealing product photos** for your eBay listings. In many cases, shooting an item against a solid black background is the best choice. (We use a felt fabric background.)

- **Learn to write appealing eBay listings.** Include at least six photos of any item you are selling.

- **Offer free shipping with your eBay listings.** Factor the shipping cost in your reserve price.

- **Get your eBay score up.** If you don't already have an eBay feedback score of ten or more, buy inexpensive items to get your feedback score up over ten. The higher the score, the more confidence bidders have in you as a seller.

Flea Market Vendor

Almost every town and city in the US has a flea market. Some are small, held one day a week, while others are huge, with hundreds of vendors, often open seven days a week, 365 days a year

People visit these flea markets looking for things to spend money on; bargains, toys for their kids, tools for their workshop, decorating items for their home.

Vendors rent tables or booths from the flea market operator, where they display their wares and try to make sales to customers who walk by.

Some vendors do this for a living – selling at either the same flea market every day or at different flea markets as they travel around the country.

Profits vary depending on the price and quantity of items being sold, the number of people who visit the market, and how often the vendor sets up a booth or table.

Some vendors earn several hundred dollars or even thousands of dollars a week, while others barely break even.

Income Potential

As mentioned earlier, the income a flea market vendor makes will vary depending on the price and quantity of items sold. Daily sales volume is dependent on several factors, including the number of people who visit the market, the weather and the buying mood of customers.

Having the right product at the right market at the right time and price is extremely important.

Start-up Costs

Getting started as a flea market vendor usually won't cost much. You'll need to pay a table rent fee ($40 or more per day), have products to sell, have at least one folding table, and if operating outdoors and permitted by the market, a pop-up canopy to provide shade.

You'll also want a few plastic storage tubs for carrying your products and to use as extra display tables. Many flea markets are set up so you can park your RV or van behind your table or booth, and have easy access to it while you work.

In almost all cases, you will have to pay the flea market operator a table or booth fee. This can be as low as twenty dollars a day, or for very large markets, over a hundred dollars a day.

Flea Market Product Ideas

So what should you sell at a flea market? The answer depends on where the flea market is being held and the kind of people it attracts.

For example, if the market is in an area where lots of young people live, you might want to sell jewelry, t-shirts, ball caps and other items that appeal to that crowd.

If living in an area with a lot of lakes, you might want to sell used fishing lures or fishing accessories.

If you have access to vintage clothing, you might want to sell that.

Items that sell well include:

- Foreign coins – very inexpensive to buy
- Stuffed animals
- Sunglasses
- Baseball caps
- Cookies, brownies, candy
- Handmade jewelry
- Fossils, crystals, rocks

For best results, try to match what you are selling with what people who visit a particular flea market want to buy.

Tools Needed

When selling at a flea market, one of the most important things you'll need is the ability to process credit card purchases. Fortunately, if you have a smart phone, processing credit cards is easy. Just sign up with Square or PayPal Here to get their credit card processing phone accessory, and you'll be in business. With either one, you can process Visa, MasterCard, and American Express credit cards.

Find details about Square at https://squareup.com/

Find details about PayPal Here at https://www.paypal.com/us/webapps/mpp/credit-card-reader

Pros

One of the big advantages of selling at a flea market is customers come to the market looking for things to buy. This means you don't have to go out and find customers, they'll be walking by your table or booth all day.

If you have the right items for sale, you can do quite well – assuming you don't run out of inventory or energy.

I've had booths at several large flea markets and trade shows, and on our very best day we took in over ten thousand dollars in profits, selling books and software. That kind of success is rare, but it can happen.

One thing I learned from my experience as a vendor is to set up a place to sit in the shade, have plenty of water and snacks, and lots of one dollar bills to make change.

Cons

If you don't like talking to lots of people (I've had thousands approach our booth and want to talk), being a vendor at a flea market won't be for you.

There is no guarantee you'll sell anything, and there are some upfront costs (table or booth rental fee).

If it is an outdoor flea market, you'll have to deal with whatever the weather happens to be – rain, shine, dust, etc.

You have to buy, make or acquire items to sell before you set up a table, and that can cost money

If held indoors, don't expect air conditioning.

Tips for Success

- **Visit several flea markets as a customer** - see what kinds of products sell best. Then try to find a source for those kind of products.

- **Prepare for a day of selling** - you'll want a comfortable chair, good shoes, plenty of water and snacks.

- **Take a relief partner** - take someone to work the booth or table with you. That way, you can take breaks without leaving the table unstaffed.

- **Take enough inventory to meet demand** - if you've found a hot selling item, be sure to have enough of it on hand to satisfy customer demand.

- **Have clearly visible prices** – make it easy for customers to see prices.

- **Be prepared to haggle** – many customers will ask you for your best price. Be prepared to offer discounts.

- **Choose items that are easy to pack** and carry away. Soft goods are better than fragile glass or electronics.

- **Watch for thieves and shoplifters** - when your booth or table is crowded with customers, some may try to steal from you. Keep valuable inventory packed up and have expensive items attached to your table with theft proof cable.

- **Take a camera** – shoot photos of other vendors who are doing well. Learn from them on how to better present your merchandise.

- **Do your research** – you can learn a lot more about selling at flea markets from several articles found at http://www.work-for-rvers-and-campers.com/rvers-vending.html.

RV Show Vendor

If you own an RV, you probably know there are hundreds of RV shows across the country. Most of these will have booths set up where exhibitors are selling RV products or services.

In many cases, the people who are working these booths are getting paid by the manufacturers of the products they represent. They travel from show to show to sell merchandise or hand out brochures and fliers of the manufacturer's products or services.

Other exhibitors are independent operators who have found products that sell well at RV shows. They'll rent a booth at the show, stock up on inventory and hope to sell out before the show is over. Then they'll restock and go to the next show.

If you like the idea of either getting paid to attend and exhibit at RV shows or having your own booth and selling products, you could become a RV show vendor or booth operator.

Profit Potential

What you earn when selling at RV shows will depend on whether you are working for a manufacturer and getting paid a commission on sales or just getting paid an hourly wage.

Earning a commission usually pays better, but only if the product being sold is something visitors at the show want to buy.

If you are an independent operator, your earnings will depend on the profit made on each item you sell and the number of items sold, less the expense of traveling to the show and paying booth rental fees.

If selling a high-profit item like ball caps, bumper stickers, paper goods and some cleaning agents, earnings per show can exceed one thousand dollars.

Getting Started

Getting started as an RV show vendor can be as easy as getting a list of upcoming RV shows and contacting the promoter to secure a booth to sell your wares.

Another way is to visit RV shows and look for vendor booths that have 'help wanted' signs. These are sometimes found at booths looking for manufacturer reps to travel the country promoting their products.

Pros

If you like traveling to different RV shows and like the idea of working a booth at these shows, either selling products or providing information about campgrounds and RV services, this might be a good fit for you.

Cons

Working a booth at a trade show can be a lot of work. You'll often meet and talk to thousands of people during a three-day show.

There's work involved in setting up and breaking down a booth. You also need room in your vehicle to carry booth resources, product inventory, and other needed booth supplies.

Booth rental at RV shows can be expensive, and there is no guarantee that you will get any sales.

In some localities, you will not be permitted to make sales at the show. You may have to purchase a license or tax stamp to sell products.

Tips for Success

- Visit RV shows before you decide to become an RV vendor. Speak to exhibitors and ask them about the lifestyle they enjoy. Find out some of the problems they face and if they would choose to do it again.

- When you visit RV shows, take a camera and shoot photos of the booths that attract the largest crowds and sell the most products. The photos will help you decide on products to sell, booth design and booth location.

- If thinking about being an independent operator at RV shows, look for products you would feel good about selling and would provide the kind of income you need.

- Choose products that require little to no support, are easy to transport, display well, and have immediate purchase appeal.

- Sign up with a credit card processor like https://squareup.com/ so you can process credit cards when customers make a purchase.

- When viewing the schedule of upcoming shows, check the restrictions on selling before reserving a booth. Also check the expected the number of attendees to make sure exhibiting at the show will be worth your effort.

Resources

- RV Industry Association
  http://www.rvia.org/

- List of RV Shows
  http://www.rvia.org/?esid=rvshows&all=1

- Florida RV shows
  http://www.frvta.org/shows/

- RV Shows
  https://gorving.com/where-to-find/rv-shows

RV Detailing for Quick Cash

While browsing Craigslist ads for used RVs, I found one offering RV exterior detailing for twelve dollars a foot. This price included a full on-site wash and wax.

At the time, I had just purchased a used twenty-four-foot motorhome, and the previous owner had never taken the time to wash or wax it.

I didn't want to wax it myself, so I decided to try out the service mentioned in the Craigslist ad.

What I discovered opened my eyes to how some people make a pretty good living while traveling in their RVs.

I called the wash and wax guy from the Craigslist ad, and he told me that he always did the job at the customer's home and all he needed was a place to connect his water hose.

We agreed on the price and time, and he showed up on time as promised. While he worked, I asked him about his business.

He told me that he lived full time in his own small RV and whenever he needed money he would run an ad in the local Craigslist, offering wash and wax services.

He said he almost always found customers, especially in areas where there were a lot of retired people.

At his rate of twelve dollars a foot, he would earn three hundred sixty dollars for a thirty-foot RV, and almost five hundred dollars for a forty-footer.

No matter the size of the RV, he would only do one job a day, not wanting to tire himself or his partner (his wife) out while working.

He told me that he typically took on three jobs a week, and would earn about a thousand dollars – all in cash.

While the work did require quite a bit of manual labor, he enjoyed what he did and makes more than enough money to live quite well while on the road.

Income Potential

In most parts of the country, a full wash and wax for an RV or camper will be priced at twelve dollars a foot or more. In some parts of the country, the price can exceed twenty dollars a foot.

If a person averages three jobs a week, at $350 per RV, they will earn over one thousand dollars a week.

Getting Started

Getting starting offering RV detailing is pretty easy. All you need to do is run ads in the 'RVs for sale' section of the local Craigslist. You will also need a phone so potential customers can contact you.

It helps if you have a partner to help you, especially when working on larger RVs.

Tools Needed

The person who showed up to wash and wax my RV had the following tools:

- Fifty-foot water hose
- Three different metal spray nozzles for the hose
- Three plastic water buckets
- Assortment of sponges and cleaning pads
- Twelve-foot step ladder
- Gel Gloss RV Wash & Wax
- Chamois cloth & drying towels
- Glass cleaner
- Tire cleaner
- Chrome polish

Pros

Offering RV exterior detailing services is a good way to generate cash when traveling in an area where a lot of people own RVs.

Cons

Washing and waxing an RV involves a lot of manual labor. The work can be strenuous, involves climbing a ladder to wash the roof, and can take hours to complete.

You will be working outdoors, and the weather could be hot, cold, freezing or raining, and that can affect the number of jobs you can do.

In some parts of the country, there won't be enough RV owners that want or need their RVs detailed.

Tips for Success

- **Make sure you are physically able** to do the work required to wash and wax an RV. It can be very strenuous work.

- NUNITO. The ad should read something like:

Mobile RV Detailing
Complete exterior detailing of your motorhome or camper, full wash, and wax. Includes entire coach body, roof, windows, tires, and wheels. We come to your location and do the work while you watch. Prices start at $12 per linear foot. Call for details or to schedule an appointment. 941-555-1212, ask for Mark.

- **Be selective on the jobs you take**. When a customer calls, ask questions about the age and condition of the RV and what the customer wants you to do. Be wary of older or damaged RVs. Check the neighborhood using Google maps to make sure it will be safe for you to work there

- **Make sure there is a water tap available** at the customer's location. You will need it to connect your hoses to wash the RV.

- **Make sure the customer knows you expect payment in cash** when the job is completed.

- **Only use high-quality cleaners**, preferably brand names like Meguiar's or Gel-Gloss RV Wash & Wax (available at Amazon and Camping World).

- **Don't overbook the jobs.** Don't schedule too many jobs per week. Leave time for jobs that take longer than expected or weather related delays

- **Watch the weather forecasts**. Avoid scheduling jobs when rain or severe weather is forecast.

- **Take before and after pictures of the RV** you are working on. Use these in your Craigslist ads. Also use as documentation in case of a question arises about damages to the vehicle you are working on.

- **Consider packing a shade tent, chair, and ice chest** with water, so you have a place to take breaks.

- **If possible, have a partner** work with you. It'll make the job go much quicker.

- **Renew your Craigslist ad** at least once a week to bump it to the top of the listings.

- When you move out of the area, **cancel your Craigslist ad**.

Other Jobs for RV'ers

There are many companies that look for and hire RV'ers and those who live full time in their campers. Most of these jobs pay well, and the positions often include free campsites for the duration of the job.

Jobs for RV'ers are listed on several websites, including:

- **Workers on Wheels**
  http://www.work-for-rvers-and-campers.com/

- **Xscapers**
  https://xscapers.com/x-job-board

- **Cool Works**
  https://www.coolworks.com/

- **Working Couples**
  http://workingcouples.com/

- **HappyVagabonds**
  http://www.happyvagabonds.com/Jobs

- **Amazon CamperForce**
  http://www.amazondelivers.jobs/about/camperforce/

- **RV Job Line**
  http://www.rvjobline.com/subscribe.aspx

- **Sugar Beet Harvest**
  http://www.sugarbeetharvest.com/

- **Be In a Movie**
  http://www.beinamovie.com/

- **Miscellaneous Workamper Jobs**
  http://www.rv-camping-lifestyle.com/workamper-jobs/

Affordable High-Speed Internet

As I promised earlier in this book, this is the chapter where I show how to get fast, reliable and secure internet all the time, with unlimited data for a very affordable twenty dollars a month.

Until recently, having a high-speed internet connection while on the road meant either parking and finding a public wi-fi signal or doing without until you reached your camp site. Even then, you weren't always guaranteed a fast and secure internet connection. Sometimes you had to pay extra for internet and more often than not the signal was weak or slow, and almost always insecure.

But with recent developments, all that has changed.

Now, with a small investment in a ZTE Mobley mobile wifi hotspot device and the $20 a month, unlimited data Connected Car plan from AT&T, you can get secure high-speed internet with unlimited usage from just about anywhere in the US – even in a moving vehicle.

The Details

A few years back, GM began offering OnStar in some of their cars. The OnStar service was essentially an internet-on-demand connection via AT&T's phone network built into the car. Access to the connection was limited to the OnStar service.

Recently, GM expanded the service by offering GM car owners unlimited internet via AT&T through the OnStar service for $20 a month. This would allow vehicle occupants to stream audio and video and connect to the web while the vehicle was in motion. This service was primarily aimed at kids in the back seat so they could be entertained by the web while the front seat occupants enjoyed the ride.

AT&T decided that rather than restrict unlimited mobile data to just GM's OnStar customers, they would offer it to everyone who asked for it. To manage this new plan, they created the Connected Car division.

Instead of needing OnStar, AT&T customers could purchase a ZTE Mobley wi-fi hotspot device and have unlimited internet in their vehicles. To make this even more attractive, AT&T offers the ZTE Mobley device for free if customers sign a two-year connected car contract.

To repeat, that's twenty dollars a month for unlimited high-speed, secure internet.

The Secret Sign Up Process

The problem with AT&T's Connected Car unlimited data plan, is most AT&T locations and retailers don't know about it. If you buy a ZTE Mobley device in an AT&T store and ask for the Connected Car Unlimited Data Plan for $20 a month, they'll say it doesn't exist.

But it does exist, I've signed up for it and have been using it for several months. You can see a screen shot of my AT&T on the next page.

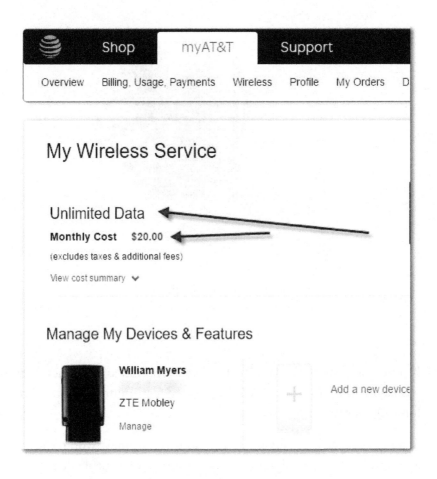

As shown in my bill, I pay twenty dollars a month (plus taxes) to get unlimited internet data on the ZTE Mobley device which AT&T provided free with the plan.

You can find the ZTE Mobley device at some AT&T Mobile stores, some Best Buy Stores, and at https://www.att.com/devices/zte/mobley.html.

ZTE Mobley wifi hot spot device

If purchasing the ZTE Mobley at a retail location, ask whether they can sign you up for the AT&T Connected Car unlimited data plan for $20 a month.

Some AT&T & Best Buy stores can do this, but most won't know about it. In that case, sign up for smallest data plan available for the ZTE Mobley device. Then after you leave the store, call AT&T Car Connect at 866-595-1222 and ask to have your current data plan switched to the 'Connected Car unlimited data plan for $20 a month'.

You will be asked for your ZTE Mobley phone number (which will show up on the receipt from AT&T). You may also be asked for the IMEI number which you'll find on the back of the ZTE Mobley device.

The sign-up process will take about twenty minutes, and when completed, you'll have the Connected Car unlimited data plan for $20 a month.

Getting connected

The ZTE Mobley device is designed to connect to and get power from the ODBC port in your vehicle. This port is usually found under the dash near the steering wheel.

However, because it can be inconvenient to find and connect to the ODBC port in your vehicle, you may want to purchase an ODBC-to-12 volt or USB adapter. You can find these on eBay for around thirty dollars (search for ZTE Mobley adapter).

The one I bought lets me connect the ZTE Mobley device to any 12-volt outlet in my motorhome.

After you have the ZTE Mobley device powered up, wait thirty seconds, and then enable wi-fi on your computer. On the list of available networks, choose to 'connect' to the one shown as ATT-Mobley. You'll be asked to enter a password – use the wifi password printed on the back label of your ZTE Mobley device. This will connect your computer or mobile device to the ZTE Mobley hotspot.

From that point, it's just like being connected to the internet through any other wi-fi network. You can browse the web, view videos, check social networks, and do whatever you need to do online.

Speed and reliability

Running speed tests on the wi-fi hotspot created by the ZTE

Mobley, I consistently get 25mbps download speed, and 20mbps upload speed – which is almost as fast as cable internet. I've never had a problem getting or staying connected, even in remote campgrounds in Florida's Everglades.

Because the plan offers high-speed internet and unlimited data, I no longer have to rely on public wi-fi. I have full-time internet in my motorhome, which I can use to connect to five devices at the same time (e.g. laptop computer, Kindle reader, my wife's tablet, and Pandora radio).

The connection works whether I'm parked or rolling down the highway at cruising speed.

What unlimited internet means

Having reliable and affordable high-speed internet anywhere you travel, can be a godsend to those of us who work while on the road. It means we are no longer limited to staying in places that offer internet, nor do we have to seek out parking lots and try to connect to random and possibly insecure public wi-fi services.

Having this high-speed wireless internet from AT&T for only $20 a month really changes the way we travel and the kind of work we can do on the road.

Notes:

1. You **do not** need to be an existing AT&T customer to sign up for this plan. Nor do you need to move your phone service to AT&T. This is a stand-alone plan.

2. While the plan says unlimited data, AT&T has the right to slow the service after you reach 20 gigabytes of data usage a

month.

3. It is likely that Verizon will offer something similar. However, at this time, they have nothing that matches the AT&T unlimited data plan.

4. I signed up for the two-year plan because I wanted to be locked into the $20 a month unlimited data, should AT&T decide to raise the price or discontinue the plan.

Hit the road and start earning

As shown in this book, there are many ways to earn a living while on the road. Regardless of your age, your physical health or your business skills, there are opportunities for you to make money while living a mobile lifestyle.

Not every method mentioned in this book will suit you and your skill set, but some will and those are the ones you should try first.

If in doubt, start out by getting a Workamper job at a campground. That way, you'll have a place to stay for free with full hook ups. Then in your spare time, try some of the techniques covered in this book.

If you do that, it won't be long before you are earning enough money to live well while on the road.

Thanks for reading. And if you should see me at your next campsite, come by and say hello.

Bill Myers

Other Books by Bill Myers

Here are other books you might be interested in:

Buying a Used Motorhome - How to get the most for your money and not get burned

Convert your Minivan into a Mini RV Camper

Mango Bob - novel

Mango Lucky

Mango Bay

Mango Glades

Mango Key

Mango Blues

Metal Detecting Florida Beaches (DVD)

Did you like this book?

Did you like this book? If so, I need your help.

I would appreciate it tremendously if you would take a few minutes to leave a review. Just a sentence or two stating that you liked the book is all it takes.

Think of it on leaving a tip after a meal you've enjoyed. Fewer than 2% of reader leave reviews.

Please be the Exception.

Thank you.

Bill Myers

Made in the USA
Monee, IL
01 December 2020